N I C K   F A W

Worship through the seasons
Reflective Services for
Special Sundays

Kevin
Mayhew

First published in 2002 by KEVIN MAYHEW LTD
Buxhall, Stowmarket, Suffolk IP14 3BW
Email: info@kevinmayhewltd.com

The material in this book first appeared in *No Ordinary Man 1* and *2,*
Are You Listening?, *To Put It Another Way*, *The Unfolding Story*,
Prayers for All Seasons 1 and *2*, and *Daily Prayer*.

9 8 7 6 5 4 3 2 1 0

ISBN 1 84003 873 X
Catalogue No 1500491

Cover design by Angela Selfe
Edited by Katherine Laidler
Typesetting by Louise Selfe

Printed in Great Britain

CONTENTS

Foreword   5

Week of Prayer for Christian Unity   7

Mothering Sunday   19

Christian Aid Week   32

Father's Day   44

Harvest Thanksgiving (1)   55

Harvest Thanksgiving (2)   64

One World Week   73

All Saints' Day (1)   85

All Saints' Day (2)   98

Remembrance Sunday (1)   112

Remembrance Sunday (2)   122

Church Anniversary (1)   131

Church Anniversary (2)   142

Appendix   152

FOREWORD

Few issues are more contentious in the Church today than worship. Its importance, in the minds of many, far outweighs theological, doctrinal or denominational differences. For some, the very idea of straying from tried and trusted patterns is tantamount to heresy. For others, those patterns have become associated with lifeless formality and, in consequence, abandoned. Personally, I believe we must make room for both, respecting and building on tradition but at the same time being open to new ideas.

One such idea I experimented with during my ministry was using meditations (often accompanied by music and slides) to bring out the meaning of Scripture. My aim was to engage the senses in a way that would capture the imagination of those participating in worship, breathing fresh life into old and familiar passages, and offering insight into the not so familiar. In time, the various meditations I wrote for such services found their way into print, under the title *No Ordinary Man*.

My purpose in *No Ordinary Man* (and its sequel *No Ordinary Man 2*) was very simple – to encourage people to reflect on the person of Jesus. I did not set out to provide answers so much as to provoke questions; to get people asking: 'Who was this man?' 'What did he do?' 'Why did he do it?' Above all, 'What does he mean for me today?' Each meditation explored such questions from the perspective of particular biblical characters that met with Jesus, either in person or through his Spirit – people like Mary and Joseph, Simon Peter and Mary Magdalene, John the Baptist and Paul. The first part of both books comprised one hundred such meditations; the second gave outlines for services and Quiet Days.

This compilation draws from *No Ordinary Man 1* and 2, *Are You Listening?*, *To Put it Another Way*, *The Unfolding Story*, *Prayers for All Seasons 1* and 2, and *Daily Prayer*. It brings together in one book a variety of services for special occasions within the Church calendar, the majority of which are not covered by the Christian Year. There is a service for Mothering Sunday, the Week of Prayer for Christian Unity, Christian Aid Week, Father's Day and One World Week, and two services each for Church Anniversary, Harvest, All Saints' Day and Remembrance Sunday. Each service comes complete with suggested readings, meditations and prayers, together with suggestions for hymns. Unlike the first two books in this series (one covering Advent and Christmas and the other Lent, Holy Week and Easter), I have not expressly included music and slides within the services, suitable material being difficult to find for the majority of occasions, but I have indicated at the beginning of each service how a visual element coupled with music might usefully be included.

If you do make use of slides and music, there are obviously certain basic requirements. A good hi-fi system, slide projector and screen are essential, as is an effective amplification system so that readers' voices carry over any background music. You will also find the services of an assistant invaluable when it comes to presenting the material – ideally somebody to control the slide projector, and possibly someone to fade the music in and out as appropriate. Remember, too, to ensure that those reading the meditations are given proper time to prepare beforehand, and that they are instructed to read slowly and clearly, beginning by announcing the title of the meditation.

Slide collections are not easy to find nowadays. You may be able to buy some from Rickett Educational Media Ltd (01458 253636) but many, sadly, are out of print. Your best bet may be to borrow them from your local Diocesan Resource Centre if you have one. Failing that, try your local library. When using slides always run through them beforehand making sure they are the right way up and in the correct order. Make sure also that you have a spare bulb in case one should blow, and arrange all electrical leads so that no one can inadvertently fall over them. The less you leave to chance, the less possibility there will be of anything going wrong.

A reflective service based around meditations represents a very different style of worship from that most people are used to, but perhaps because of this it may be able to bridge the gap between the diverse contemporary patterns and understandings of worship, and, more important, speak to those who may not usually contemplate attending church. If this book even begins to achieve that, then it will have served its purpose.

NICK FAWCETT

Week of Prayer for Christian Unity

Possible visual and music material

Transparencies of the Last Supper from the slide series *Jesus of Nazareth* or *The Life of Christ IV* could usefully be used in this service. More originally, you could take your own transparencies of various church buildings and congregations within your town and set these to a piece of music such as 'Jesus, you are the way' from *Fountain of Life* by Margaret Rizza. See Appendix (page 152) for details.

Introduction

We have come together from different churches, representing various emphases in faith yet as one people in Christ. Whatever may divide us, we are reminded today that much more unites us through him. Today we look back at the words of Jesus concerning that unity and we consider too the experience of divisions within the early Church, asking what things keep us apart and what bind us together.

Hymn

The Church's one foundation is Jesus Christ her Lord
Let there be love shared among us

Prayer of praise

Loving God,
    we have come together in this place sharing the same faith,
    yet we are all different,
    each of us unique.
Though we are many, you have made us one.
Together, we praise you.

We have different experiences and interpretations of faith,
    yet we are bound by the same goal
    and united by the same Lord.
Though we are many, you have made us one.
Together, we praise you.

We praise you for the things that make us what we are –
    the experiences that have shaped us,
    the memories that are our own,

the backgrounds from which we come.
Though we are many, you have made us one.
Together, we praise you.

We praise you that faith is not something learned by rote
    or inherited by birth,
    but our own,
    each of us having a story to tell –
    a story of life;
    a story of faith.
Though we are many, you have made us one.
Together, we praise you.

We praise you for the community that binds us together,
    the fellowship we share in Christ,
    the mission he has given us,
    the love he has put in our hearts,
    the hope we have in common.
Though we are many, you have made us one.
Together, we praise you.

We praise you for everything we are able to share together –
    the rich heritage of the Church,
    the inspiration of examples of faith,
    the insights of different traditions,
    the challenge of diverse experiences.
Though we are many, you have made us one.
Together, we praise you.

Loving God,
    help us to learn from one another,
    never closing our minds to the diversity of your Church.
Help us to grow in faith day by day,
    knowing your love and goodness for ourselves.
Help us to share what you have done for us,
    and to listen to all you have done for others.
So may our faith be deepened and our service enriched,
    as we continue along our individual pathway of faith
    and on our pilgrimage together.
Though we are many, you have made us one.
Together, we praise you.
Through Jesus Christ our Lord.
Amen.

Comment

To hear Christians talk, sometimes, you would think that there was a time when everything in the Church was sweetness and light – no differences of opinion, no divisions, no clashes threatening to tear things apart. The reality, of course, could hardly be more different; from the very beginning all kinds of tensions surfaced posing a continual threat to the Church's future. I suspect, though, that such tensions were present even earlier, for when you look at those Jesus called to be his disciples, it is hard to imagine that never a cross word was spoken between them. They were, as we shall explore further in the following meditation, an unlikely mixture of people to inaugurate a life-changing movement, and yet they were to do just that. How? Because God had called them together in Christ, and that continues to be the only way in which those whom God calls to be his people can hope to live and work together for his kingdom. We are indeed all different, but in Christ we share the same faith and serve the same Lord.

Reading: Mark 10:35-45

Meditation of Peter

I had no doubts at the beginning,
    not when he first called me.
There was something about the man –
    the authority in his voice,
    the honesty in his eyes –
    that made it almost impossible to say no.
He was unique,
    I was certain of that immediately;
    the sort of man you could trust,
    stake your life on if necessary,
    and I believed if anyone was worth following,
    anyone quite clear what they were all about,
    it was Jesus.
But I'm not sure now,
    not sure at all,
    for he's just come back with a new bunch of recruits,
    and, honestly, you ought to see them –
    a motley crew if ever there was one!
There's this chap Matthew for a start –
    a tax-collector of all people! –
    he's really going to win us some friends, isn't he?
Then there's Simon, the so-called Zealot –

well, we've all heard about him –
a right rabble-rouser by all accounts;
you can bet your last shekel that when there's trouble brewing,
rebellion in the air,
he'll be there in the thick of it.
To be fair, I can't say yet about the others, but I have my doubts,
especially Judas –
a bit of a snob, if you ask me,
too full of himself by half.
And Thaddeus? Well, he's just the opposite –
a nobody really,
quiet as a mouse –
I can't see him making much of an impression.
Nor Bartholomew for that matter.
So what's Jesus thinking of?
I just don't know.
It's shaken me, I don't mind telling you.
Don't misunderstand me, I'm still happy to follow Jesus,
no question about that,
but I don't want to get mixed up with this lot.
Why couldn't he have stuck to fishermen –
decent, honest, sensible folk like us?
Why complicate everything,
involve people from different backgrounds
with a different way of looking at life?
We knew where we stood at the beginning,
just James, John and me, together with Jesus.
If he needed others, there were plenty more we could have recommended,
friends and colleagues we could guarantee would never rock the boat.
But now who's to say what might happen?
I suppose he knows what he's playing at, even if I can't see it yet.
Maybe he knows something about these fellows that I don't,
maybe he has some purpose in mind which I haven't quite understood.
So fair enough, I'll go along with him,
for the moment anyway,
despite my misgivings.
He obviously wants us to work together,
obviously thinks we can too.
Well, we'll see.
Time will tell, won't it?
But if it's going to work it will need a miracle, that's all I can say.
An absolute miracle.

Prayer

Lord Jesus Christ,
 some people are easy to get on with,
 others are hard;
 we are naturally drawn to some,
 but shy away from others;
 there are some we enjoy working with,
 others who constantly rub us up the wrong way.
Yet you have called us into a family in which all have their place,
 however different they may be.
Teach us to see our differences as strengths,
 and help us to be ready to learn from one another,
 for your name's sake.
Amen.

Hymn *Lord of the Church, we pray for our renewing*
      Come, all who look to Christ today

Comment

There are some who see moves towards Christian unity as incidental to what we should be about, and a few who are even hostile to any attempt to draw the Church together, regarding any but themselves or those of a similar theological disposition as suspect if not altogether unsound. Yet to think like this is to fly in the face not just of reason but of Christ himself, for as the following reading and meditation remind us, one of his final wishes was that the Church should be one, its unity serving as a living witness to his love.

Reading: John 17:9-23

Meditation of John the Apostle

We were there in the upper room,
 just us and Jesus,
 the night drawing in,
 the end drawing near.
We knew it,
 he knew it.
There could be no doubt any more, not for any of us,
 no question of a last-minute reprieve.
We'd seen Judas sneaking out, darkness in his eyes,
 and we knew it wouldn't be long before the vultures descended,

hungry to devour their prey.
We wanted him to run for it –
    back to Nazareth,
    back to Galilee,
    back to the safety of the wilderness;
    anywhere but there in Jerusalem.
But he wouldn't listen, of course,
    wouldn't even consider it.
So we stayed with him,
    nervous,
    fearful,
    one eye over our shoulders, but determined to do our best for him.
He was under no illusions;
    he knew full well what was coming –
    an ugly, agonising death.
And it was getting to him,
    eating away inside,
    that much we could all see.
When he broke bread, he was trembling,
    clearly petrified about what lay ahead;
    and as he shared the wine, there was a sob in his voice,
    a tear in his eye.
Yet then he spoke,
    softly,
    gently,
    almost as if in a dream,
    and we realised he was praying –
    not for himself,
    but for us,
    not for his life,
    but the life of the world!
Yes, I know that sounds hard to believe, but it's true, honestly –
    I was there, remember,
    I heard him.
It wasn't the prospect of death that was troubling him;
    it was the fear that we wouldn't stay together,
    that somehow we'd become divided,
    even end up fighting among ourselves.
God knows why he thought that –
    I've no idea where he got the idea from –
    but you could see how worried he was,
    how much our unity meant to him.

It was his dying wish in a way,
    his last request –
    that we should stay together:
    one people,
    one faith,
    one God.
I'm sure he needn't have worried, least of all at a time like that.
All right, so we've had our differences since, I admit it –
    we don't always see things the same way,
    and maybe once in a while we might even fall out –
    but I honestly can't imagine anything major coming between us, can you?
Not in the long run.
After all, we're his disciples, aren't we, each one of us –
    all called by him,
    all confessing the same Lord,
    and what could ever be more important than that?

Prayer

Lord Jesus Christ,
    your body was broken for us.
You endured the agony of the cross to reconcile us to God,
    to break down the barriers that divide us,
    to make us one.
Forgive us that we have erected new barriers in place of old,
    barriers that divide us from one another,
    that separate church from church and Christian from Christian.
Help us to recognise that you died not just for some but all of us,
    and help us to understand that nothing that may keep us apart
    can be more important than the truth that binds us together.
Amen.

Hymn   *Bind us together, Lord*
             Brother, sister, let me serve you

Comment

In our next two readings and meditations, we turn to Paul's first letter to the Corinthians, a letter dominated by issues of controversy and contention. Here, more than anywhere, we see the divisions in the early Church laid bare, and in the Apostle's determination to counter these we see the importance he placed upon Christian unity. Arguments concerning spiritual gifts, theology and worship continue to scar the Church today as deeply, if not more so, as denominational divides. We will all shake our heads at such discord, but, of course, its seeds lie deep within us all, for it is an innate human tendency to prefer our own way of doing things, to believe that we are right and others are wrong. The Week of Prayer for Christian Unity is not just a time to pray for unity, but equally one that calls us to search our hearts honestly, and to recognise within ourselves that which so often and so easily separates us from one another.

Reading: 1 Corinthians 1:10-25; 12:12-13, 25-27

Meditation of Paul
If he could see us now, what would he think?
It would break his heart, I'm sure of it,
　　cause him as much pain, if not more, as those nails in his hands,
　　that spear in his side.
How could they do this to him?
After all he said,
　　all he did,
　　all he tried to teach us!
I can't believe it's happening,
　　that we could be so stupid.
But it is,
　　and we can.
I've seen it,
　　right here in Corinth;
　　heard it with my own ears;
　　and what hurts most is that I'm involved –
　　like it or not, I'm a part of it.
We're divided,
　　split up into our own little factions,
　　and it's happened without us even noticing it.
'I'm for Apollos,' says one;
　　'I'm for Peter';
　　'I'm for Paul.'
And I know this is just the beginning;
　　that there will be more –
　　other leaders,
　　other teachers –
　　each with their own little band of followers.
What *have* we done,
　　and where do we go from here?
I'd like to say we can sort it out,

bury our differences and get on with what really matters –
after all, we're all rooting for Christ, surely?
That's what it's all about,
that's who we claim to follow –
Christ crucified and risen!
Folly to some perhaps,
nonsense to others,
but to us the power and wisdom of God!
Yet it's not that simple, of course –
I know that as well as any –
for what does that actually mean –
for me,
for you,
for others?
That's when the trouble starts,
the rifts appear,
for we're all different,
each one of us –
each with our own unique experiences,
our individual way of looking at things,
our particular quirks and foibles.
I soon found that out,
stunned to find those I counted as brothers and sisters in Christ
opposing my work,
actually condemning my preaching to the Gentiles.
There are no easy answers, sadly,
no magic solutions,
and yet we have to work this thing out somehow;
we can't just sit back and accept it,
for I'm telling you, it would break his heart if he could see us now.
If!
What do I mean, *if?*
He *can* see it!
He *is* seeing it!
And every day it continues we carry on crucifying him –
our divisions,
our separation,
pinning him to that cross in agony!

Silent reflection

Reading: 1 Corinthians 11:17-22; 12:1, 4-6, 12, 27-31

Meditation of Paul

It was all so unnecessary,
    such a senseless stupid waste –
    grown men and women who should have known better,
    arguing amongst each other,
    almost coming to blows,
    and all over so-called gifts of the Spirit.
Well, some gifts they turned out to be!
I could hardly believe it,
    so much anger,
    so much bitterness,
    just because people experienced God differently.
Why couldn't they see the other's point of view,
    recognise that some need to express themselves one way,
    some another;
    some have this gift,
    others one completely different?
Why turn it into a competition,
    a test of spiritual blessing?
It wouldn't have been so bad had it been over something important –
    our failure to love,
    our inability to forgive,
    our weakness in discipleship.
But this –
    it was all finally so trivial,
    the whole business peripheral to what should really have concerned us.
Oh, I don't deny such things have their place –
    a time and a season for everything –
    but when they divide rather than bring together,
    upset rather than uplift,
    surely something has to be wrong somewhere?
Yet they just wouldn't have it,
    each vying to outdo the other,
    jostling to claim the most spectacular gift,
    the profoundest blessing.
Couldn't they see the damage they were doing,
    the message they broadcast to the world?
Didn't they realise that every dispute, every division
    broke again the body of Christ,
    inflicting yet more suffering upon him?
Apparently not.
They were tearing themselves apart,

slowly but surely destroying the unity
   which he had suffered such agony to bring them,
   and all in the name of his Spirit.
Don't think I blame one above the other.
I don't.
They were all at fault,
   each as intolerant as the next,
   denying through their deeds what they claimed with their lips.
It's up to them now –
   I've done my best,
   tried to get the message home.
They can go on feuding if they want to,
   no place for anyone but themselves,
   but when the day comes when they're finally called to account,
   and they find then that there's no place for anyone like themselves,
   don't say I didn't warn them!

Prayer of intercession

Lord Jesus Christ
   we pray today for your Church,
   conscious of the issues that still divide us,
   our failure to enjoy the oneness you desire.
Wherever your body is broken today,
   make us one, Lord.

We pray for Christians who feel threatened
   by contrasting patterns of worship,
   diverging expressions of faith,
   and conflicting theological positions;
   rejecting those they do not agree with as unsound
   rather than risk engaging in genuine dialogue.
Give them openness to other points of view.
Wherever your body is broken today,
   make us one, Lord.

We pray for fellowships that have been torn in two,
   split by controversies over doctrine and churchmanship,
   divided over issues of faith and worship,
   or undermined by petty disputes.
Instil in them a spirit of healing and reconciliation.
Wherever your body is broken today,
   make us one, Lord.

We pray for denominations involved in moves towards greater unity,
    striving to overcome years of separation
    but finding themselves tied down by procedure and practicalities,
    frustrated by bureaucracy and tradition.
Grant wisdom and insight, so that obstacles may be overcome.
Wherever your body is broken today,
    make us one, Lord.

Lord Jesus Christ,
    reach out to your Church
    and work in hearts everywhere,
    to break down barriers,
    to overcome prejudice,
    and to bring people together in genuine love and understanding.
Wherever your body is broken today,
    make us one, Lord.
In your name we ask it.
Amen.

Hymn   *Blessed be the tie that binds*
             Lord, from whom all blessings flow

Closing prayer
Living God,
    open our hearts to one another
    through opening them to you,
    and so send us out,
    as one people,
    in the name of Christ.
Amen.

Mothering Sunday

Possible visual and music material You may perhaps be able to find a slide or slides of Jesus welcoming the little children, or you could arrange for a set of transparencies to be taken of mothers and children within your own church, and show these, set to music (such as 'Come to me' from *Fountain of Life* by Margaret Rizza – see Appendix, page 152), at one point during the service (perhaps after the third meditation).

Introduction We are here today to think of mothers – of what they mean to us or have meant. We are here to think of motherhood and of those denied its joy. We are here to think of children, celebrating all they bring to us in so many ways. Above all, we are here to think of God, and to reflect on what we can learn of him from the relationship between a mother and child. As we focus today on those who gave us birth, so we respond also to the one who offers new birth and new life to all.

Hymn *Now thank we all our God*
Come, let us sing of a wonderful love

Prayer of praise

Gracious God,
  on this special day of thanksgiving,
  we catch a glimpse, through a mother's love for her child,
  of your love for us;
  the care, dedication and devotion you show to all your children
  which makes you as much 'our Mother' as 'our Father'.
For that great truth
  we praise and thank you.

We owe our very lives to you.
You have watched over us from our birth,
  tenderly nurturing us,
  showering us with love.
When we have needed you, you have been there.
For that great truth
  we praise and thank you.

You have given us strength in times of need,
    comfort in times of distress,
    encouragement in times of despair,
    guidance in times of uncertainty.
Whatever we have faced, you have been with us.
For that great truth
    we praise and thank you.

Gracious God,
    we have not always appreciated your love,
    all too often ignoring what you would teach us,
    disobeying your instructions,
    taking you for granted and wandering far from your side.
Yet through it all your love has remained constant.
For that great truth
    we praise and thank you.

Gracious God,
    Mother and Father of us all,
    caring for us more than you care for yourself,
    sacrificing your all for our sakes,
    loving us with an unquenchable love,
    you have called us all to be your children.
For that great truth
    we praise and thank you.
In the name of Christ.
Amen.

Reading: 1 Corinthians 13:1-3

Comment

Few words crop up more often in terms of the Christian faith than 'love', but what does it mean? The answer, of course, is many things, but the love God has for us is of a special intensity; a love that perhaps is nowhere glimpsed better than in the relationship between a mother and child. The following meditation takes that relationship as its starting point, and asks the question, 'How far do we truly love?'

Meditation (to be read by two voices)

Lord, I saw a photograph today,
 a picture of a mother desperately shielding her baby from a hail of bullets,
 sacrificing herself to protect her little one.
And there I saw love,
 total love –
 not the pale imitation we pass off in its place,
 but the real thing,
 concerned only to give,
 pouring itself out, oblivious to the cost.
I admired that, Lord,
 and I longed to share it.
No, not the pain and sacrifice, not that,
 but the ability to love with even a fraction of that selfless devotion –
 for I know deep down that I don't.
I speak of love often enough –
 sign off with it in a letter,
 send it casually over the phone –
 but it's just a word,
 well-intentioned but hollow.
And even with those dearest to me,
 my friends and family,
 though I care deeply about them, more than they will ever know,
 my love is still imperfect,
 as much about *me* as them –
 my happiness,
 my desires,
 my wishes,
 my well-being.
I'm not good at loving, Lord,
 and that troubles me, for it strikes at the very heart of my faith.
Love your enemy, love your neighbour, love one another –
 isn't that what you tell us to do?
And it all sounds wonderful,
 a recipe for heaven.
But it's one thing to bandy such fine words as theory –
 I do it all the time –
 it's another to mean them, let alone to make them real.

My child,
 it's quite true what you say –
 love *is* difficult,

more costly and demanding than most people ever imagine;
and it's true also that your love is less than it ought to be,
as much about yourself as others.
But that's not so terrible,
for I tell you this:
unless you learn to love yourself
you will never love anyone else.
Besides, there is more to you than you give credit for.
That picture you speak of, the mother shielding her child –
you're not so different, despite what you think.
You too could rise to that same devotion and commitment,
that same willingness to sacrifice all.
It would take a lot, I grant you,
and I hope you'll never be put to the test,
but there are those you care about enough to die for them if necessary.
Believe me, I know,
for I care that much about you, about everyone,
only it cost me more still –
the cruellest of agonies,
the most unimaginable pain.
I came to this world in Jesus,
sharing your human suffering,
bearing your grief and sorrow,
and out of love I watched him give everything,
nailed to the cross so that you might live.
It was dreadful,
harder than you will ever know not to step in and call a halt –
my child far too precious to die like that.
But I held back, honouring his wishes,
as he laid down his life for all.
So, yes, it's difficult, love – I understand that,
but it's not impossible, not now anyway,
for it's been given freely,
in the blood of my Son shed for you –
and when love like that flows through your veins
it must surely soon beat in your heart.

Hymn   *Great God, we sing your guiding hand*
In heavenly love abiding

Reading: Luke 1:5-23

Comment

If this day brings joy to some, it also brings pain to others. There will be those whose mothers or children have died, those orphaned as youngsters or coming from broken homes, those who have become estranged, and, finally, those like Elizabeth and Zechariah who endure the pain of child-lessness. For these, this day adds to their trauma, reminding them of shattered hopes and abandoned dreams. We need to remember them too, and to pray that they especially will know the reality of God's everlasting arms encircling them and his love holding them close.

Meditation of Zechariah

I didn't believe it was possible any longer,
    not after all those years of trying.
There had been so many disappointments,
    so many false alarms,
    and we'd given up, ages ago.
It still hurt occasionally, of course it did –
    we love children, both of us,
    and we'd have given anything to see that little crib occupied,
    that lovingly embroidered shawl wrapped around our little baby.
We shouldn't have tempted fate –
    it was stupid, we know that now –
    but at the time we never anticipated any problems
    and we just couldn't help looking forward, planning for the future:
    two bright-eyed young things with so much before us,
    or so we thought.
She used to cry, Elizabeth,
    after her hopes had been raised only to be dashed again,
    and although I'd try manfully to comfort her,
    assure her next time it would be different,
    all the while my heart was breaking as much as hers.
But then she started to torture herself,
    feeling she'd failed me somehow,
    that it was all her fault,
    even God's punishment for some unrepented sin.
I don't need to tell you she was wrong,
    but it was hard work making her see that –
    so much extra heartache
    before she finally accepted it was just one of those things.
But then I had this dream –

at least I think that's what it was.
I was in the temple
    and suddenly a man appeared telling me we were to have a child,
    ordained by God and consecrated to his service, so he said.
Well, I dismissed it, of course –
    a cruel trick of the mind, I thought –
    but the next thing I knew there was Elizabeth,
    a look of wonder in her eyes,
    blurting out the news that she was expecting!
Well, you could have knocked me down, you really could!
I honestly thought she was having me on,
    that the strain had finally got to her,
    but I couldn't say anything –
    I'd been struck dumb since that dream of mine –
    so I just stood there, trying to humour her.
I'm glad now I couldn't speak, pour scorn on the idea,
    for she was right.
A child, at our time of life!
I still marvel every day I see him,
    our wonderful little boy,
    and I know now never to lose hope
    for with God nothing is impossible.
Yet we were the lucky ones, I realise that,
    and for every one of us there's another still enduring the pain,
    still waiting, hoping and praying for a miracle.
I don't know why God lets that happen
    any more than I know why he chose to bless us;
    it's a mystery to us both.
But there's an odd twist I have to mention,
    for though our baby brought us joy,
    more than words can ever express,
    somehow Elizabeth seemed even more excited
    by the birth of her cousin's boy –
    Jesus the name was –
    always claimed he was more of a miracle than John,
    though I can't think why.
She's no nearer understanding this crazy world of ours than I,
    but when she looks at Jesus
    sometimes I get this strange feeling that it's in him,
    rather than John,
    that she's looking for an answer;
    almost as though she expects him to make sense of it all.

Silent reflection

Prayer

Gracious God,
　　on this Mothering Sunday we bring you our prayers
　　for all entrusted with the responsibility of motherhood.
Loving Lord,
　　hear our prayer.

We pray for mothers the world over,
　　recognising both the joys and demands they experience –
　　the privilege and pressures,
　　hopes and fears,
　　pleasure and pain that motherhood entails.
Equip them with the love, wisdom and strength they need.
Loving Lord,
　　hear our prayer.

We pray for single mothers,
　　bearing the responsibility of parenthood alone,
　　struggling sometimes to make ends meet,
　　and stigmatised by certain sections of society.
Grant them the emotional, physical and financial resources they need.
Loving Lord,
　　hear our prayer.

We pray for mothers who have experienced heartbreak –
　　their children stillborn or seriously disabled,
　　injured, maimed or even killed through accident or assault,
　　struck down by debilitating disease or terminal illness.
Comfort them in their sorrow.
Loving Lord,
　　hear our prayer.

We pray for those denied the joy of motherhood –
　　enduring the trauma of infertility,
　　prevented on health grounds from risking a pregnancy,
　　or simply unable to establish a relationship
　　into which children can be born.
Help them to come to terms with their pain.
Loving Lord,
　　hear our prayer.

We pray for those who foster or adopt children,
    those who long to do so but who are denied the opportunity,
    and those who for various reasons have given up their children
    and are haunted by the image of what might have been.
Grant them your strength and support.
Loving Lord,
    hear our prayer.

We pray finally for those who long to discover their natural mothers,
    those who have become estranged from them
    and those whose mothers have died –
    all for whom Mothering Sunday brings pain rather than pleasure,
    hurt rather than happiness.
May your love always enfold them.
Loving Lord,
    hear our prayer.

Gracious God,
    we pray for mothers and children everywhere.
May your blessing be upon them,
    your hand guide them
    and your love enrich them all.
Loving Lord,
    hear our prayer.
Through Jesus Christ our Lord.
Amen.

Hymn   *O love, how deep, how broad, how high!*
            Love divine, all loves excelling

Comment

We have considered the example set by mothers and thought of those denied the joy of motherhood. We turn now to children, and to their special qualities that Jesus held up as an example to all who would enter his kingdom. His taking of a child in his arms is not just an endearing story designed to warm the heart; it was a symbolic action intended to challenge the soul.

Reading: Mark 10:13-16

Meditation of Andrew

I could have brained those children,
    rushing around like that with their yelling and shrieking,

shattering our peace and quiet.
We'd had him alone at last,
    just us and Jesus;
    a rare opportunity to sit and listen undisturbed,
    drinking in his every word.
And it was wonderful,
    a truly magical moment,
    until, that is, they turned up,
    those wretched kids ushered forward by their doting parents,
    just so that he could touch them.
Really, how ridiculous!
Superstition, that's all it was –
    no real faith behind any of it –
    just sentimental rubbish,
    nauseating!
So we tried to stop them; you can understand that, surely?
We wanted to get back to the business in hand,
    before we were so rudely interrupted;
    back to more serious matters.
OK, so maybe we were a bit over the top,
    a touch more heavy than the situation demanded,
    but we were angry,
    disappointed.
I mean, could *you* have concentrated with that row going on?
I couldn't.
Yet did they care?
Not likely!
We fully expected Jesus to back us up,
    send the lot of them packing.
But can you believe this? He didn't!
He actually turned on us,
    and there was anger in his eyes,
    anger touched almost with pity.
'Leave them alone,' he said. 'Let them come to me. What's your problem?'
Well, we didn't know what to say, did we?
It caught us right on the hop.
So we just fidgeted uncomfortably, trying to cover our embarrassment.
It was so unfair.
We'd meant no harm, after all,
    certainly hadn't meant to upset anybody;
    yet there they were now,
    the kids bawling their eyes out,

the mums looking daggers at us,
   the dads having a go at everyone.
What a mess!
I honestly didn't know what to do next,
   but thankfully Jesus came to the rescue as always.
He reached out and took the children in his arms, one by one,
   and then he lifted them up for all to see.
 'These are special,' he told us,
   'more precious than you will ever know –
   each one treasured by God.'
And you could tell from the way he smiled at them
   that he meant every word he was saying,
   and from the way they smiled back at him that they knew it full well.
I still feel a bit aggrieved by it all –
   well, you can tell that, can't you –
   but I realise now we made ourselves look rather silly that day,
   even childish, you might say;
   and I'm beginning to understand Jesus has no room for the childish;
   only the childlike.

Silent reflection

Hymn   *Christ who welcomed little children*
             Love is his word

Comment

We turn finally to the love God has for us, a love as deep, passionate and totally committed as that of a mother for her child. Nowhere is that more beautifully expressed than in the words of the prophet Hosea, where God is pictured pouring out his grief at the repeated rejection and betrayal of his people. Here is an unforgettable glimpse into a love that refuses to let go despite everything that is thrown against it. There may be several pictures in the New Testament to rival it; there are few that more eloquently express God's love for us and all his people.

Reading: Hosea 11:1-9

Meditation of Hosea

I never realised how much he cared,
   how deeply and passionately he loved us.
He'd seemed remote up till then,

set apart from us in splendid isolation,
    a God to approach with caution.
Not that I ever questioned his goodness –
    he'd been gracious to us from the beginning,
    calling us into being as a nation,
    delivering us time after time from oppression,
    leading us with infinite patience
    despite our refusal to follow –
    but I'd always had this picture of him as being distant,
    a God whose face we could never see,
    sovereign,
    righteous,
    holy,
    and, ultimately, a little frightening.
When we came to worship, we did so in awe,
    and as we knelt in prayer, we approached with trepidation,
    knowing he could judge as well as bless,
    punish as well as save –
    and let's face it, after the way we'd behaved
    there was every reason for punishment,
    and none at all for mercy.
We'd worshipped false gods,
    pale reflections of our own fears and fantasies,
    instead of the Lord of heaven and earth.
We'd oppressed the poor and exploited the weak,
    let greed run riot and vice go unchecked.
We'd said one thing and done another,
    spoken of justice yet practised deceit,
    so what reason to expect anything other than judgement,
    due recompense for all our sins?
Only he couldn't do it!
When the moment came to reach out and punish, he drew back,
    heart lurching within him –
    the memories too strong,
    his compassion too great,
    love refusing to be denied.
It wasn't any personal merit that saved us, don't think that,
    some hidden virtue uncovered or past deed recalled.
We'd failed him completely,
    spurning his goodness and abusing his grace,
    yet, despite it all, he refused to let us go.
And I realised then that,

holy though he is,
still he loved us, more than we can ever begin to imagine;
a love that will keep on giving,
keep on burning
and keep on reaching out for all eternity,
whatever it may take,
whatever it might cost!

Silent reflection

Prayer of confession

Gracious God,
    we are reminded today of how easily we take a mother's love for granted,
    failing to express our thanks for the care we receive,
    slow to demonstrate our appreciation
    for the patient nurture given over so many years.
For forgetting to show our gratitude,
    Lord, forgive us.

We are reminded equally of how easily we take *your* love for granted,
    failing to thank you for the blessings *you* shower upon us,
    the care with which you daily surround us
    and the joy with which you fill our lives.
For forgetting to show our gratitude,
    Lord, forgive us.

We have assumed that words do not need saying,
    that our thankfulness can be taken as read.
We have believed love comes easily,
    failing to recognise what it can sometimes cost.
We have imagined because no thanks is asked that no thanks is necessary.
For forgetting to show our gratitude,
    Lord, forgive us.

Gracious God,
    help us to understand the joy we can bring through saying thank you,
    not just today but every day,
    not just to our mothers but to everyone,
    and not just to everyone but to you.
And help us, through the act of thanksgiving,
    to recognise how much we have to be thankful for.

For forgetting to show our gratitude,
Lord, forgive us.
In the name of Christ we ask it.
Amen.

Hymn   *O love that will not let me go*
         The King of love my shepherd is

Closing prayer

To the one whose goodness is without equal,
    whose love is beyond comparison,
    whose mercy is beyond understanding,
    and whose power is beyond words,
    be praise and glory,
    worship and thanksgiving,
    now and always.
Amen.

CHRISTIAN AID WEEK

Possible visual and music material Christian Aid supplies various slide sets that could usefully be used in this service, either with accompanying text or set to music.

Introduction 'Not everyone saying to me, "Lord, Lord" will enter the kingdom of heaven, but rather those who do the will of my heavenly Father' (Matthew 7:21). These words remind us, like few others, of the need to match faith with works, words with deeds. Unless we practise what we preach, or at least attempt as best we can to do so, our commitment is exposed as hollow and the gospel held up to ridicule. This week reminds us of that same need. The work of Christian Aid speaks of the concern of Jesus for the poor and of his promised kingdom in which there will be justice for all. The fulfilment of that promise is yet to come, but we cannot abdicate the present through putting all our hopes in the future. We have a responsibility here and now to work towards a better and fairer world, living and giving sacrificially in the name of Christ. Today, then, we reflect on words and promises of Jesus that ask us quite simply: how far does our faith show itself in action?

Hymn *God's Spirit is in my heart*
Sing we a song of high revolt

Prayer of praise

Lord Jesus Christ,
    we remember that you came to turn the world upside down –
    to scatter the proud in the imagination of their hearts;
    to bring down the powerful from their thrones
    and to lift up the lowly;
    to fill the hungry with good things
    and to send the rich away empty.
For the dawn of your kingdom,
    and all who work towards its fulfilment,
    we praise you.

We remember that you came to bring good news to the poor;
    to proclaim release for the captives
    and recovery of sight to the blind;
    to let the oppressed go free
    and to proclaim the year of the Lord's favour.
For the dawn of your kingdom,
    and all who work towards its fulfilment,
    we praise you.

We remember that you came to bring healing to the sick
    and strength to the weak,
    hope to the despairing
    and comfort to the broken-hearted,
    joy to the sorrowful
    and succour to the suffering.
For the dawn of your kingdom,
    and all who work towards its fulfilment,
    we praise you.

We remember that you came to judge with righteousness
    and to decide with equity for the meek of the earth;
    to bring love where there is hatred,
    peace where there is war,
    and life where there is death.
For the dawn of your kingdom,
    and all who work towards its fulfilment,
    we praise you.

Lord Jesus Christ,
    we remember, too, that you come again, day by day,
    in the hungry and thirsty,
    the stranger and the sick,
    the naked and the imprisoned;
    your voice calling out for food and water,
    for acceptance and compassion,
    for clothing and concern.
We thank you for all who respond to your call,
    striving to build a better world.
Inspire us through their service,
    and teach us to respond in turn.
For the dawn of your kingdom,

and all who work towards its fulfilment,
   we praise you.
Amen.

Comment

Faith and works: we can so easily divorce the two – but from the start Jesus made it clear that they belong together, his words concerning the kingdom of God emphasising the place of justice and good news for the poor. The gospel was not just about spiritual fulfilment and eternal life, though those were certainly central features. It was also about hope, acceptance, freedom and dignity for all; about life now as well as the life to come. As he stood up to speak in the synagogue in Nazareth, he left his listeners in no doubt that we divorce religion from the needs of our world at our peril.

Reading: Luke 4:16-30

Meditation of a member of the Nazareth Synagogue

He had a wonderful voice,
   a real joy to listen to;
   so clear,
   so deep,
   so nicely-spoken.
I felt I could have sat there all day,
   letting the words wash over me –
   good news for the poor,
   release for the captives,
   recovery of sight for the blind –
   familiar,
   comfortable,
   reassuring words.
Or so I'd always thought,
   only this time they didn't sound quite as reassuring as they used to.
I don't know what it was,
   but somehow as he spoke they came to life,
   possessed of a power they had never held before,
   as if I were hearing them for the very first time,
   only the prophet was speaking not to people long ago,
   but to me,
   here,
   now.

And suddenly I didn't want to hear,
    didn't want to listen any more,
    for the words were no longer what I'd thought they were,
    but unexpected,
    discomforting,
    troubling words.
They leapt at me and pinned me down.
They lunged at me piercing my very soul.
They left me anxious,
    guilty,
    fearful,
    asking what they meant to someone like me
    who was neither poor nor blind,
    but rich and free.
I closed my ears
    but still he spoke,
    and, listening again, despite myself, I heard him say,
    'A prophet is without honour in his own country.'
That was the end,
    too much,
    the voice no longer seeming beautiful but strident,
    no longer bringing joy but rousing rage,
    for I realised this man came not to soothe but to challenge,
    not to praise but to question.
I rose in rage, an ugly mob beside me,
    cursing him for his blasphemy,
    calling for his death!
Yet somehow, he slipped through our fingers,
    unharmed,
    untouched.
Don't ask me how, for I just don't know,
    but what I do know is this, much though it hurts to admit it:
    when Jesus told us,
    'These words have been fulfilled today in your hearing' –
    he was right
    and I was wrong.

Silent reflection

Hymn   *Where cross the crowded ways of life*
             God of freedom, God of justice

Comment

What does it mean to serve God and respond to Christ? There are, of course, many answers to that, each of which has its place. Christian Aid Week, however, reminds us of one answer in particular that we sometimes under-play and may even at times overlook. It speaks of the simple act of caring, of responding to people in their need, irrespective of creed or culture. Too easily, we relegate such concern to the periphery of faith, preferring to focus on supposedly more 'spiritual' issues, but the words of Jesus concerning the sheep and the goats offer a different perspective, placing our response to others not on the edge but at the very centre of faith. We listen to his words, and then hear two meditations exploring their implications.

Reading: Matthew 25:31-46

Meditation of Matthew

He told us he would come again,
    that as he had departed so he would return.
And we believed him,
    totally,
    without reserve or hesitation.
It kept us going, that promise,
    the one thing that gave us strength to battle on through thick and thin.
Yet sometimes,
    just occasionally,
    I catch myself wondering whether we should look forward;
    whether it will all be so cosy,
    so comfortable,
    as we sometimes seem to imagine.
You see, I can't help remembering those words of his,
    about the sheep and the goats,
    about the final judgement –
    so simple,
    so straightforward,
    yet so chilling in their implications:
    'I was hungry, and you fed me,
    thirsty, and you gave me a drink,
    a stranger and you welcomed me,
    naked, sick, imprisoned, and you were there to help.'
That's what he said –
    through serving these,

even the very least of them,
 you serve me.
It sounds good, doesn't it,
 the sort of message we like to hear.
Yet sometimes those words disturb me,
 for I can't help asking, 'Which am I?'
Oh, I know which I'd like to be, stands to reason! –
 and I know which I should be, all too well.
But if I'm honest,
 really truthful with myself,
 I fear I'm more often a goat than a sheep.
I saw the plight of the hungry,
 but it was me I worried about feeding.
I heard the cry of the thirsty,
 but it was my own need I satisfied.
I spotted the loneliness of the stranger,
 but wasn't sure I could trust them.
I was told about the naked,
 but it was I who got the new clothes.
I glimpsed the despair of the sick,
 but was afraid to risk infection.
I knew some were denied their freedom,
 but was reluctant to get involved.
Not now, I told them;
 next time I'll do something,
 next time I'll help,
 God will understand.
But will he, that's the question?
I've been good at talking,
 good at preaching,
 good at praying,
 and in faithfulness at worship I have few peers.
Yet when I recall those words of Jesus
 and measure them against his life,
 sometimes I find myself almost hoping he doesn't come back,
 for if he does and judgement comes,
 even though I've called him Lord,
 it may be me at whom he points the finger,
 and me he says he never even knew.

Silent reflection

Meditation of two Christians on the day of judgement
(To be read by two voices, alternately)

I wasn't much of a Christian, the way I saw it.
(*I wasn't a bad Christian, the way I saw it.*)
Test me on doctrine and I'd be lost completely,
(*Test me on doctrine and I'd have a ball,*)
    the complexities of theology a mystery to me.
    (*the niceties of theology a delight to me.*)
My prayer life?
(*My devotional life?*)
That wasn't much better,
(*That was spot on,*)
    the words somehow never seeming to flow,
    (*the words coming so easily,*)
    discipline hard to achieve.
    (*discipline coming naturally.*)
It was the same with the Bible, I'm sorry to say;
(*It was the same with the Bible, I'm glad to say;*)
    I found most of it a closed book.
    (*I knew it inside out.*)
I tried hard enough, heaven knows,
(*I hardly had to try,*)
    but, let's face it, it's not the easiest of books to read,
    (*for, let's be honest, it's such a wonderful book to read,*)
    so many passages serving to puzzle rather than inspire.
    (*every passage seeming to leap out and speak to me.*)
And, as for obedience, well, the less said about that the better,
(*And, as for obedience, well, I'm not one to boast,*)
    for I kept slipping back into my old ways,
    (*only it was as though my old self had died completely,*)
    temptation catching me unawares,
    (*temptation brushed aside,*)
    my relationship with God a shadow of what it should have been.
    (*my relationship with God everything it could be.*)
So you can see what I mean, can't you? –
(*So you get my point, don't you? –*)
    not much of a Christian, all told,
    (*not a bad Christian, all told,*)
    and as I stood there before Jesus, I feared the worst,
    (*and as I stood there before Jesus, I had no fears whatsoever,*)
    uncertain of his verdict, to say the least.

(confident of his verdict, to put it mildly.)
You can imagine my relief, can't you?
(You can imagine my shock, can't you?)
'Come, you that are blessed by my Father.'
('Depart from me . . . you that are accursed.')
I couldn't believe my ears!
(I thought I was hearing things!)
What had I done to deserve such blessing?
(What had I done to deserve such punishment?)
When had I ever put myself out for Jesus?
(When had I ever let Jesus down?)
Yet I *had*, time and again, without ever realising it.
(Yet I had, *day after day, without ever realising it.)*
When I reached out to the needy,
(When I turned my back on the needy,)
   when I responded to the poor,
   (when I ignored the poor,)
   when I visited the sick,
   (when I recoiled from the sick,)
   I was serving Jesus, easing his pain, expressing his love.
   (I was failing Jesus, adding to his pain, denying his love.)
I'm not much of a Christian, I still think that,
(I wasn't a bad Christian, I really believed that,)
   yet, happily, I got one thing right –
   (yet I got one thing hopelessly wrong –)
   I responded to others,
   (I put myself before others,)
   I showed I cared,
   (I didn't care,)
   and now love brings its own reward.
   (and now I must pay the price.)
God moves in mysterious ways.
(God have mercy on me, a sinner.)

Hymn   *Where restless crowds are thronging*
              The law of Christ alone can make us free

Comment

Do only committed Christians serve Jesus? Not according to the parable we've been focusing on. Indeed, many may serve him unawares, while those of us who profess his name may abjectly fail him through our neglect of others. Don't let that happen. We can claim no monopoly of love or goodness, but we are those who should constantly strive to express Christ's love in action. As he himself put it, we are called to be salt of the earth. The phrase is familiar, but what does that actually mean, and, more important, how far is it true of you and me?

Reading: Matthew 5:13

Meditation of Zebedee, a Galilean fisherman
Salt.
You can't get much more ordinary than that, can you?
We've got masses of the stuff,
    enough in the Dead Sea alone to supply the world's needs,
    I shouldn't wonder!
So when Jesus turned to us the other day
    and told us, 'You are the salt of the earth',
    you can well appreciate why I scarcely batted an eyelid –
    it was hardly the highest accolade he could have given, was it?
At least, that's what I thought then,
    only now I'm having second thoughts,
    for it's struck me since just how much we use salt for:
    preserving,
    purifying,
    seasoning,
    even healing wounds on the odd occasion –
    such remarkable properties for so commonplace a substance.
It's one of those things we take for granted, isn't it? –
    until we haven't got it,
    and then, suddenly, we realise how much it's needed,
    how vital a role it has.
Is that what Jesus was saying to us –
    that our role, too, is to preserve and purify,
    to bring a little extra sparkle and spice into life,
    to help heal this bleeding broken world of ours?
Not in any pretentious way,
    blowing our own trumpet or parading our virtues,
    but quietly,
    without fuss,
    our contribution barely noticed
    yet indispensable nonetheless,
    the world a poorer place without our service?

It's a thought, isn't it? –
    inspiring,
    daunting,
    breathtaking,
    humbling –
    though it's hard to believe;
    the idea of us making even half such an impact
    quite frankly seeming incredible.
Yet just imagine if we could;
    what a ministry that would be!
And, come to think of it, isn't that precisely what we see in Jesus,
    his life lived for others,
    his way of unassuming service,
    gently yet irrevocably transforming the world?
I was wrong, wasn't I,
    for in that simple illustration
    he paid us the highest compliment possible
    and issued the most awesome of challenges.
'You are the salt of the earth' –
    you can't get much more special than that, can you?

Prayer of confession and intercession

Gracious God,
    as we come to you on this Christian Aid Sunday
    we are conscious that we are the lucky ones –
    those with food in our bellies and a roof over our heads,
    with ample supplies of water and medicine,
    with access to education and technology,
    our lives brimming over with good things.
You have given us so much.
Teach us to give generously in turn.

We pray then for the millions less fortunate than us –
    those for whom hunger is a daily reality,
    a proper home a luxury,
    fresh water, medical care and education a dream,
    and the lifestyles we enjoy here a source of wonder and bewilderment.
You have given us so much.
Teach us to give generously in turn.

We pray for organisations like Christian Aid,
    giving you thanks for their work

for their courage to stand out against injustice,
striving to build a fairer world despite powerful opposition
and frequent misunderstanding.
Give them strength to continue their work,
and give us the will to support their cause,
not just once each year in Christian Aid Week,
but every day,
through the lives we live,
the sacrifices we make,
and the faith we proclaim.
You have given us so much.
Teach us to give generously in turn.

Gracious God,
forgive us that it takes a day like Christian Aid Sunday
to turn our thoughts to the poor.
Teach us to live for others throughout our lives,
and to work towards the fulfilment of our prayers
through the things we do
and the people we are.
You have given us so much.
Teach us to give generously in turn.
In the name of Christ.
Amen.

Hymn   *Yesu, Yesu, fill us with your love*
For the healing of the nations

Closing prayer
In the brokenness of our world, God is there.
In the cry of the hungry,
the suffering of the sick,
the plight of the homeless
and the sorrow of the bereaved,
he is calling your name.
In the misery of the lonely,
the despair of the oppressed,
the plea of the weak
and the helplessness of the poor,
he is seeking your help,
asking for your response.

The world is bleeding,
  and God is bleeding with it,
  waiting for your hands,
  your care
  and your love
  to help heal the wounds.
As you have come *to* him,
  now go *for* him,
  in the name of Christ.
Amen.

FATHER'S DAY

Possible visual and music material
Why not arrange for a set of transparencies to be taken of fathers and children within your own church, and show these, set to music such as the *Meditation* by Massenet, at one point during the service (perhaps after the third meditation)?

Introduction
'Our Father, who art in heaven' – the words are so familiar that we scarcely give them a second thought, and yet they embody one of the most marvellous truths of the gospel: the fact that we can indeed refer to God as 'our Father'. Although we are talking about the Creator of the ends of the earth, the one who is all good and all pure, before and beyond time, still he calls us his children. Although his ways are not our ways or his thoughts our thoughts, he wants us to enjoy a personal relationship with him. Here is one of the unique facets of the Christian faith that makes it so special. The Lord of heaven and earth, the God beyond, loves us as deeply and devotedly as a father loves his child. As we give thanks today for fathers and fatherhood, let us also give thanks for the God who invites us to call him 'Abba, Father'.

Hymn *Our Father God, thy name we raise*
I lift my eyes, to the quiet hills

Prayer
Sovereign God,
  Creator of the heavens and the earth,
  ruler over space and time,
  we praise you that we can respond to you as a father;
  that we can approach you,
  not in a spirit of subservience or fear,
  but as your children,
  assured of your love and secure in your purpose.
Father of all,
  we worship you.

We praise you that you care for us as much as any father cares for his child
and far more besides –
your hand always there to guide and discipline,
to provide and protect,
to comfort and encourage,
to nurture and cherish.
Father of all,
we worship you.

We praise you that your love is inexhaustible –
that, however often we fail you,
however many times we may stray from your side,
you seek us out,
striving to restore the relationship we have broken,
always ready to forgive and forget.
Father of all,
we worship you.

We praise you that we are made in your image,
capable of understanding good and evil,
able to appreciate treasure in heaven
as well as the many riches of this world,
and able also to respond to your love in Christ
and so inherit your kingdom.
Father of all,
we worship you.

Sovereign God,
we come to you on this Father's Day,
giving thanks for everything that fathers mean to us,
but rejoicing, above all, in your fatherly care for all.
With grateful hearts, we bring you praise
and commit ourselves again to your service.
Father of all,
we worship you.
Through Jesus Christ our Lord.
Amen.

Comment

When it comes to the fatherhood of God, surely few pictures are more
wonderful than that painted in the parable of the lost son. We tend to
read the story from the perspective of the son as he comes to realise the

folly of his ways, but listen to it now putting yourself in the position of the father, and consider what it is saying about the nature of God.

Reading: Luke 15:11-32

Meditation of a lapsed Christian returned to faith
Lost and found!
It wasn't the first parable he'd told on that theme,
    but to me it was the best,
    those words of his, when I heard them read,
    falling like music on my ears,
    for though the message was much the same as before,
    the implications were so very different.
I was just like that young man, you see,
    the second of the two sons,
    not simply lost but having wilfully gone astray.
I'd known and understood the Father's love,
    what it was to be part of his family,
    and I'd gone and frittered it all away,
    preferring my way to his,
    squandering the riches he'd given me,
    living with no thought of his will or guidance.
It was my own doing, no one else's.
I'd plumbed the depths of despair,
    sunk until I could sink no lower,
    and it was all down to me,
    a self-made humiliation.
That's what frightened me the most:
    to be lost is one thing –
    anyone can make a mistake –
    but to be the knowing instrument of your own destruction,
    to recognise the error of your ways and carry on regardless,
    can God forgive that?
I thought he'd washed his hands of me,
    that if I dared approach him he'd shake his head
    and tell me, 'I told you so',
    so I kept my distance and lived with my shame as best I could.
Only, suddenly, here was Jesus speaking not just of forgiveness
    but joyful acceptance,
    a love reaching out to meet me,
    celebrating my return,
    welcoming me home,

and it dawned on me that the mercy of God
is greater than I'd ever begun to contemplate.
I'd walked away,
   thrown his gifts back into his face,
   and I'd assumed there could be no return.
But I was wrong,
   for he was there waiting,
   longing to receive me back,
   arms outstretched to hold me close.
I was lost,
   and now I'm found!

Silent reflection

Comment

'Would any among you, should your child ask for bread, give a stone? Or if asked for a fish, would you give a snake? If then, you who are flawed, know how to give good gifts to your children, how much more will your heavenly Father give good things to those who ask him' (Luke 11:11-13, author's paraphrase). So said Jesus in his teaching to the disciples on prayer, and in those words is a reminder of a God who delights to give good things to us, to grant his blessing whenever and wherever he can. How different this is from the remote angry being we sometimes make God out to be. Here instead is a loving Father longing to bring happiness to his children. Never be afraid to approach God, for he is always ready to listen and always looking to respond.

Reading: Luke 18:1-8

Meditation of Peter, one of the twelve disciples

There was so much I wanted to ask,
   so much I longed to bring before God in prayer,
   yet, somehow, I just couldn't bring myself to do it.
Does that sound strange to you?
It should do,
   though if you're anything like I was
   you'll understand well enough.
You see, it was God we were talking about here,
   the Creator of heaven and earth,
   above and beyond all,
   Alpha and Omega,
   sovereign in his holiness –

who was I to dare approach such a one?
He had other matters to attend to,
   other business of more pressing concern,
   and, even if he found time,
   what interest could he have in a miserable wretch like me –
   stubborn,
   wilful,
   disobedient,
   just about as far removed from him as it's possible to be?
So that was that,
   my dealings with God, such as they were,
   carried out at arm's length,
   with no suggestion of meaningful dialogue
   or a personal relationship.
It took that outrageous parable of Jesus to teach me sense –
   a contrast so ridiculous yet so obvious
   that even I had to sit up and take notice.
For he was right, wasn't he?
Even the worst of us,
   the most unfeeling, uncaring and unjust have our threshold,
   a point at which, for the sake of peace if nothing else,
   we hear someone out and respond to their plea.
And if that's true with us, then where does it leave God,
   the one we call good,
   gracious,
   compassionate,
   slow to anger and swift to bless,
   full of justice and righteousness,
   rich in mercy and abounding in steadfast love?
How can we say all that and still hold back,
   still imagine he does anything else but delight in our prayers
   and hunger to grant our requests?
I forget that sometimes, even now,
   the old idea of God still rearing its ugly head,
   but, when that happens, I think again of those words of Jesus,
   I picture that judge cursing
   as, reluctantly, he grants the woman's request,
   and then I offer my prayer,
   confidently,
   joyfully,
   without reserve,
   knowing that he is there as always –

our Father! –
ready to listen,
ready to speak,
ready to touch my life and grant again his blessing!

Silent reflection

Hymn   *Father, hear the prayer we offer*
           Father in heaven (or any other adaptation of the Lord's Prayer)

Comment

There are some people in whose presence we feel the need to be on our best behaviour. We feel that every word and action is being scrutinised in case it causes offence or fails to measure up to what's expected. Indeed, there's a sense in which all of us wear a mask most of the time, and there are few people in front of whom we are ready truly to be ourselves. To do that requires total love and trust. God, we are told, is such a one, before whom we can let down our defences, knowing that he accepts us and loves us as we are. He may want us to change, but his love is not conditional on that. He reaches out day after day, offering his grace, guidance and support. Though we may reject him, he will not reject us.

Reading: Romans 8:12-17

Meditation (to be read by two voices)

It's me, O Lord –
    not the person I pretend to be,
    nor who I want to be,
    but me, as I am,
    with all my strengths,
    all my weaknesses,
    all my faith,
    all my doubt –
    me, as I've rarely dared come before,
    reaching out to you in prayer.
I've no right to be here, I know that,
    for I'm nothing special,
    nothing to write home about,
    and I've little idea what I'm going to say,
    still less how to say it.
But you tell us if we truly seek, we shall find,
    if we're really sorry, you'll forgive,

if we keep on asking, you will answer.
So I'm here, Lord,
    in all my ugliness and sin –
    weak,
    selfish,
    greedy,
    thoughtless –
    but I'm here,
    and I'm asking you, despite it all:
    hear my prayer.

My child,
    don't stop,
    keep talking,
    for I'm here too,
    delighted to listen,
    drinking in your every word.
It's a joy to hear you, believe me,
    music to my ears –
    no need to apologise or excuse yourself.
I've looked forward to this moment for so long,
    your coming openly and honestly to meet me.
For it's *you* I want to talk to,
    not the mask you wear for the world –
    you as you really are –
    the face you show, the face you hide,
    the person you love, the person you hate.
They're both you,
    two halves of the same whole,
    inseparable as light and dark, substance and shadow,
    and unless you bring all, openly and honestly before me,
    you bring nothing.
You're not perfect, I know that,
    but I don't ask you to be –
    it's not me who twists the knife, only you.
I love you as you are,
    with all your faults and fragile faith,
    and I'll go on loving you day after day,
    drawing you closer to me
    not as a condition but an expression of that love.
So come now, gladly and confidently,
    bring yourself with head bent low but soul held high,

and find in me your kindest critic
and truest friend.

Silent reflection

Comment

We began by noting that the God who is sovereign over all astonishingly invites us to call him Father, and it is to that idea we finally return, listening to one of the best-known and best-loved of all the psalms that emphasises both his farness and nearness. Here, once more, is the God before whose magnificence we catch our breath in wonder, and before whose love we catch our breath in praise.

Reading: Psalm 139:1-18

Meditation of David

It's no good, Lord,
   it's too much for me,
   more than I can ever take in.
I've tried, you know that.
Day after day I've struggled
   to get my head round the wonder of who and what you are,
   but I just can't do it;
   your greatness is beyond the reach of human mind.
I've come far, no question,
   new insights and experiences adding to my sense of wonder,
   deepening my faith,
   enlarging my vision;
   yet I realise now that those were just a taste,
   a small sample of what is yet in store,
   for there is always more to learn,
   much that is hidden still to be revealed.
It's frightening, almost,
   for you overturn all our expectations,
   at work not just in the light, but in the darkness,
   not just in the good, but in the bad –
   no place outside your purpose
   no person beyond your grace,
   your love stronger, wider, greater, deeper
   than I've even begun to imagine!
Always you are there,
   one step ahead,

waiting to take my hand
and lead me on to the next stage of my journey.
So that's it, Lord.
enough is enough –
no more tying myself into knots,
no more juggling with the impossible.
I don't have all the answers
and I never will have,
but I've got you, here by my side,
behind to guard me,
ahead to lead me,
above to bless me,
within to feed me –
your love always there,
every moment,
everywhere,
in everything.
And, quite honestly, if I've got that,
what else do I need to know!

Silent reflection

Prayer of intercession
Father God,
we pray today for those entrusted with the responsibility of fatherhood,
all who have the duty and privilege of raising children,
fashioning their lives,
offering a stable and loving environment in which they can grow,
leading them along the exciting yet demanding path to adulthood.
Grant them love, insight and devotion.
Father of all,
hear our prayer.

We pray for fathers whose marriage or relationship with their partner
has broken down,
separated from their children or seeing them only occasionally,
many having responsibilities for another family,
and we pray also for stepfathers
who will fill the role that once was theirs.
Grant them commitment, dedication and sensitivity.
Father of all,
hear our prayer.

We pray for fathers with no sense of responsibility,
    failing to make time for their children,
    careless in offering support and guidance,
    casual in providing discipline,
    abdicating their role as parents.
Grant them forgiveness,
    repentance and the opportunity to make amends.
Father of all,
    hear our prayer.

We pray for children of broken homes,
    deprived of a father figure
    or knowing first one, then another,
    rarely able to establish a meaningful and lasting relationship.
Grant them stability, support and the knowledge that they are still loved.
Father of all,
    hear our prayer.

We pray for children abused by their fathers,
    emotionally scarred for life,
    struggling to come to terms with their experience,
    haunted by an image of fear rather than love.
Grant them healing, peace and courage to face the future.
Father of all,
    hear our prayer.

Finally, we pray for those who have lost their fathers,
    whether as children or as adults,
    for some their father little more than a name,
    for others a heart-wrenching memory,
    but each carrying a sense of loss.
Grant your strength, your comfort and your hope.
Father of all,
    hear our prayer.

Father God,
    we lift before you today fathers and their children.
Enfold them in your love,
    and surround them with your fatherly care,
    today and every day.
Father of all,
    hear our prayer.
Through your Son, Jesus Christ our Lord.
Amen.

Hymn   *Father, I place into your hands*
              Lead us, heavenly Father, lead us

Closing prayer

To God who is higher than our highest thoughts,
    yet closer than our closest friend,
    be thanks and praise,
    glory and honour,
    this day and for evermore.
Amen.

Harvest Thanksgiving (1)

Possible visual and music material

For this service, ask members of your congregation for any transparencies they may have relating to the countryside (for example, sunsets, flowers, mountains, pastoral views, animals, seascapes, waterfalls). Show these at one or various points during the service, set to such pieces of music as *What a wonderful world* sung by Louis Armstrong, 'The Swan' from the *Carnival of the Animals* by Saint-Saëns, 'In Paradisum' from Fauré's *Requiem*, or the 'Shepherd's Song' from Beethoven's *Pastoral Symphony*.

Introduction

Across the years, as Harvest so powerfully reminds us, few things have spoken more eloquently of God's presence than the wonder of creation. We should not, of course, idealise nature, for there is much within it that is harsh and even ugly, yet this can never detract from the loveliness of so much around us: the awesomeness of the stars at night, the simple yet exquisite beauty of a bird singing or bud bursting into bloom, the evocative smell of the sea or scent of a wild flower. These speak not just of the wonder of this world but also of the splendour of God. We celebrate today the beauty of so much that surrounds us, and alongside that we consider our place within it all.

Hymn   *Come, you thankful people, come*
Jesus is Lord! Creation's voice proclaims it

Prayer

Loving God,
　we come this day to praise you,
　to celebrate your great goodness.
We come with thanksgiving, joy and wonder,
　reminding ourselves of the richness of your creation,
　and acknowledging your faithfulness
　in providing for all our needs and far beyond!
You have blessed us beyond our deserving,
　gladly we rejoice.

Loving God,
    for the beauty of the seasons,
    the constant cycle of day and night,
    and the vital gifts of rain and sunshine,
    we praise you.
You have blessed us beyond our deserving,
    gladly we rejoice.

For the miracle of growth,
    the wonder of life,
    and the incredible variety of harvest,
    we bring you our thanksgiving.
You have blessed us beyond our deserving,
    gladly we rejoice.

Receive then our worship,
    accept our offerings,
    bless our celebration,
    and fill us with thankfulness for all you have given.
You have blessed us beyond our deserving,
    gladly we rejoice.
In the name of Christ.
Amen.

Reading: Psalm 96:10b-13; 147:7-9, 15-18; 148:1, 3, 5, 9-10, 13

Comment

In those words we catch a sense of wonder at the rich variety of God's creation, the beauty of the natural world around us, and it is this same sense that lies behind the two meditations that we shall now hear, the first following on from those passages we have just heard, and the second picking up the words of Jesus concerning the flowers of the field, as well as words once again from the book of Psalms.

Meditation (to be read by two voices)
I'll never forget it, Lord,
    the moment I stood on that hilltop
    and took in the sight before me –
    the sun golden on the horizon,
    the sea stretching out into the distance, blue as topaz,
    the cliffs white as snow,
    and the seagulls soaring overhead in lofty splendour.

It was magnificent,
    a taste of paradise,
    the world as I'd never seen it before,
    full of beauty and wonder.
I heard cows lowing and sheep calling their young,
    birds singing in the distance and bees droning among the heather,
    the laughter of the waves
    and the playful whispering of grass stirred by the breeze,
    each joining to create a jubilant chorus,
    an outpouring of celebration,
    a hymn of praise.
And my heart joined in the dance,
    leaping with delight,
    skipping with pleasure,
    crying out in adoration.
For here was freedom and inexpressible loveliness,
    life as it ought to be,
    creation in all its glory.
It was wonderful, Lord,
    a glimpse of your majesty,
    a revelation of your handiwork,
    a sign of your love –
    and in that moment, as never before, I gave you my worship.

My child,
    this may come as a surprise,
    but that moment was precious to me as well as you,
    for the wonder in your eyes and the joy in your face
    was a prayer greater than all words,
    an expression of gratitude I shall always treasure.
So thank you for your worship,
    and thank you for taking time to stop and stare,
    to glimpse my presence in the beauty of creation,
    to reflect on my handiwork and know me by your side.
Don't lose that sense of awe,
    for it is a gateway to heaven,
    a foretaste of my eternal kingdom.
Yet remember also there is more to discover –
    that if you found me once in a moment of quietness,
    you must find me always in every place and every moment.
Make time to withdraw, of course,
    but then return,

back to the daily round of life.
Make time to pause,
    but then resume,
    picking up where you left off.
Make time to reflect,
    but then to act,
    seeing my presence in the place where I have placed you,
    for when you have learned that, my child,
    we shall dance together for all eternity.

Silent reflection

Reading: Psalm 8:1, 3-6, 9; Matthew 6:28-29

Meditation (to be read by two voices)
It was beautiful, Lord,
    more lovely than I'd ever begun to realise –
    a single rose,
    newly opened,
    still wet with the morning dew –
    and I stood there gazing,
    utterly enchanted by its simple perfection.
Another flower, that's how I'd seen it before,
    pleasant enough,
    attractive,
    yet hardly wonderful.
But now, as I stooped to view it closely,
    as I caught its perfume and noted each delicate petal,
    I glimpsed a miracle,
    a work of art,
    an astonishing labour of love.
And I saw you there, Lord,
    your hand,
    your presence –
    the gentleness of your touch,
    the order of your mind,
    the tenderness of your heart.
I saw your love expressed in that one fragile bloom,
    symbol of a world put together with inexpressible care –
    a world full of delight,
    able to stir our imagination and thrill our hearts,
    to move and inspire us beyond words,
    to touch our souls with a taste of heaven.

My child,
   you think it beautiful, that flower?
I'm glad, for it's meant to be,
   though all too few see it.
But if you think that's special,
   look around you at this world I've made –
   its diversity of life,
   its variety and interest,
   so endlessly complex,
   so infinitely fascinating.
Look at the sky –
   the glow of the sun,
   the twinkle of the stars,
   the vastness of the heavens.
And, most of all, look at yourself and your fellow human beings –
   your awesome array of talents,
   your incredible potential,
   the amazing miracle of human life.
Here too is beauty,
   most astonishing of all.
In the laughter of a child and the vigour of youth,
   in the embrace of lovers and the joy of parents,
   in the experience of maturity and the wisdom of age,
   I am present,
   for you are all the work of my hands,
   a testimony to my purpose,
   a reminder of my never-failing love.
So look again, my child, at that simple flower,
   at the loveliness of this world,
   only see there not just the wonder of me,
   but the wonder of you!

Silent reflection

Hymn   *God whose farm is all creation*
            Carpenter, carpenter, make me a tree

Prayer of thanksgiving and confession
Lord of all,
   we thank you for our universe with its infinite fascination,
   for our world with all its wonder.
   for our countryside with all its beauty,

for life itself in all its incredible variety.
Loving Lord,
   hear our prayer.

There is so much that gives us pleasure,
   that offers us fulfilment,
   that captures our imagination,
   that challenges and inspires,
   that gives us cause to look forward with anticipation,
   that speaks to us of your great love.
Loving Lord,
   hear our prayer.

Forgive us for so often abusing all you have given –
   for despoiling our world,
   for failing to appreciate it as we should,
   for losing our childlike sense of wonder and inquiry,
   for treating it as ours by right rather than entrusted as your gift,
   for being blind to your loving hand moving behind it all.
Loving Lord,
   hear our prayer.

Open our eyes to the countless blessings
   and inexhaustible riches you have so freely given,
   and help us to show our appreciation
   by being faithful stewards of your creation.
Loving Lord,
   hear our prayer.
In the name of Christ.
Amen.

Hymn   *O Lord my God, when I in awesome wonder*
          All things bright and beautiful

Comment

We have considered the beauty of creation and the way it speaks to us of God, but alongside the privilege of living in this world he has given us, there is also responsibility, and it is to this that we turn in our final meditation. God has given us a unique place in creation, but that does not mean, as we sometimes seem to imagine, that he has given us *carte blanche.* He expects us to act as stewards of creation, to live in such a way that we safeguard his gift for future generations. To fail in that is to betray the responsibility he has placed into our hands.

Reading: Psalm 8:1-9

Meditation of David

Is it possible?
Can it really be true that God has time for you and me?
It seems preposterous,
 stretching credulity to the limit,
 for what place can we have in the grand scheme of things;
 what reason for God to concern himself about our fate?
I look at the vastness of the heavens
 and the awesome tapestry of creation,
 and we're nothing,
 just the tiniest speck against the great backdrop of history.
And yet amazingly,
 astonishingly,
 we matter!
Not just *noticed* by God,
 but *precious* to him,
 special,
 unique,
 holding an unrivalled place in his affections and purpose.
Can it be true? –
 a little lower than God himself,
 made in his image?
It sounds fantastic,
 almost blasphemous,
 for who are we –
 weak, sinful, fatally flawed humanity –
 to be likened to the sovereign God,
 creator of the ends of the earth,
 enthroned in splendour,
 perfect in his holiness?
Yet there it is,
 incredible yet true,
 not just part of creation but stewards over it –
 the beasts of the field
 the birds of the air,
 the fish of the sea –
 their future in our hands;
 this wonderful world,
 so beautiful,
 so fragile,

placed into our keeping,
   held on trust.
That's how much he loves us,
   the ultimate proof of his care.
What a wonderful privilege!
What an awesome responsibility!

Silent reflection

Reading: Psalm 95:3-7a

Prayer of intercession
Lord of all,
   as we thank you for our harvest
   we remember those who do not celebrate –
   those whose harvest is poor or non-existent,
   those with insufficient resources to tend their land,
   those denied a just reward for their labours, the fruits enjoyed by others,
   those whose harvest has been destroyed
   in the chaos of war or natural disaster.
Lord, you have blessed us richly;
   teach us to remember others.

Help us, as we celebrate our plenty,
   to remember those who have so much less –
   the poor and needy of our world,
   driven by famine, disaster or civil war to the brink of starvation.
Help us to respond with love and concern, offering the help we can.
Lord, you have blessed us richly;
   teach us to remember others.

Lord of all,
   speak to us at this harvest time,
   so that our hearts may be stirred and our consciences quickened.
Teach us to share our bounty with those who have nothing,
   so that the time may one day come
   when all have enough and none too much.
Lord, you have blessed us richly;
   teach us to remember others.
In the name of Christ.
Amen.

Hymn   *We plough the fields and scatter*
           For the fruits of his creation

Closing prayer

Go out into the world rejoicing,
    for God is waiting to meet you
    and surprise you with the beauty of his presence.
In the song of a blackbird,
    the hooting of an owl,
    the cry of a fox;
    in the opening of a bud,
    the fragrance of a flower,
    the falling of a leaf;
    in the murmur of the breeze,
    the rushing of the wind,
    the howling of the gale;
    in the babbling of the brook,
    the rippling of the stream,
    the crashing of the waves;
    in the peace of the meadows,
    the freedom of the hills,
    the grandeur of the mountains;
    in the cry of a baby,
    the laughter of children,
    the hum of conversation;
    in the pat on the shoulder,
    the handshake of welcome,
    the embrace of a loved one;
    in the noise of the factory,
    the routine of the office,
    the bustle of the shop –
    God is here,
    God is there,
    God is everywhere.
Go then,
    and walk with him,
    in the light of his love,
    and the fullness of life.
Amen.

Harvest Thanksgiving (2)

Possible visual and music material   For this service, why not take a set of transparencies showing packets of seeds and then the full-grown plants? If you feel this is beyond you, scout around in your congregation for someone with the skills and confidence to have a go. The slides could be set to music such as 'Spring' from Vivaldi's *The Four Seasons*.

Introduction   There are two ways to approach Harvest. We can focus simply on the beauty of creation and the faithful provision of God, or we can think of it from a 'spiritual' perspective, reflecting on the harvest God wants to see in our lives and the wider world. We turn today to that second perspective, reflecting on parables of Jesus that draw on the natural world of growth and harvest. We consider the parable of the mustard seed and its lesson concerning God's ability to bring about the growth of his kingdom from seemingly unpromising beginnings. We consider the parable of the hidden seed, recognising that though we have a part to play in bringing about the harvest of lives won for Christ, we are ultimately dependent on God's grace. We look at the parable of the weed-filled wheat field, asking how far our lives are producing the crop God wants to see growing there. Finally, we turn to the parable of the barren fig tree, giving thanks for the assurance that though we may fail to yield this crop, by the grace of Christ we are constantly offered another chance to become the people he would have us be. As we worship today surrounded by reminders of another harvest, let us examine ourselves, and pray for a similar harvest of spiritual fruits in our life, and a harvest of souls throughout the world.

Hymn   *Morning has broken*
For the beauty of the earth

Prayer

Living God,
    creator of all that is, and has been, and shall be,
    we bring you this day our thanksgiving
    for everything you have given us.
You have blessed us in so much;
    teach us to use your gifts wisely.

We thank you for the infinite beauty of our world,
    for the complexity of the universe,
    for the wonder of creation that can never be exhausted.
You have blessed us in so much;
    teach us to use your gifts wisely.

We thank you for the constant miracle of day and night,
    summer and winter,
    springtime and harvest,
    the regular cycle of life that we know and depend on.
You have blessed us in so much;
    teach us to use your gifts wisely.

We thank you for the rich resources of this planet,
    and for all those who labour in different ways
    to make them accessible to us.
You have blessed us in so much;
    teach us to use your gifts wisely.

We thank you for minds with which to understand, enquire and learn,
    for senses with which to see, hear, smell, taste and touch,
    and for health to enjoy, savour and celebrate.
You have blessed us in so much;
    teach us to use your gifts wisely.

Forgive us that sometimes we lose our sense of thankfulness,
    becoming complacent and over-familiar with the richness of creation.
Forgive us for taking your many blessings for granted,
    forgetting them,
    squandering them,
    even abusing them.
You have blessed us in so much;
    teach us to use your gifts wisely.

Living God,
    give us a new sense of joy and gladness,
    and hearts that are truly thankful.
Help us to recognise again the awesome riches of creation,
    and to rejoice in the blessings which you shower upon us.
You have blessed us in so much;
    teach us to use your gifts wisely.
Through Jesus Christ our Lord.
Amen.

Reading: Mark 4:30-32

Meditation of the gardener of Joseph of Arimathea

A mustard seed!
You can't get much tinier than that, can you?
One breath,
    the faintest of breezes,
    and it's gone,
    tossed away to heaven knows where!
It's hard to believe it grows as it does,
    tall enough for the birds to build their nests in.
Yet isn't that the way life so often turns out,
    small beginnings yielding the most surprising of results?
From a gentle spring comes a mighty river,
    from a single spark a leaping flame;
    day after day it happens, if only we have eyes to see.
I shouldn't have needed reminding of that, should I,
    for, I'd seen it often enough,
    but when it came to grasping the growth of God's kingdom
    I suppose I simply never thought of it in those terms.
Foolish of me, I know,
    except that I'd been brought up to think differently,
    the picture in my mind one of some dramatic event,
    the glorious advent of the Messiah coming to claim his throne,
    splendid,
    spectacular,
    sensational,
    indisputable proof that here was the one we'd waited for –
    God's chosen deliverer sent to set us free.
So when it came to Jesus,
    for all his wonderful words and deeds I was unconvinced;
    attracted, certainly,

deeply challenged,
   yet unable to stop myself asking, 'What can God achieve through him?'
He just didn't fit the bill.
And when I saw him finally hustled before Pilate,
   condemned to death
   nailed to a cross,
   well, that seemed to be it,
   the final nail in the coffin, you might say.
Only it wasn't,
   for, like a seed entombed in the earth,
   he rose up,
   reaching out not just to us but all the world,
   the extent of his purpose beyond anything I'd imagined,
   the breadth of his love utterly breathtaking;
   and I realised that in this man
   God had worked the most staggering of miracles:
   from the child of Bethlehem, the King of kings and Lord of lords,
   from one man's death, life for us all!

Prayer

Lord Jesus Christ,
   there are times when we wonder what we can possibly do
   to advance your kingdom or further your will.
We feel hopelessly inadequate for the task before us,
   our resources so small,
   our gifts so few,
   the idea that we can achieve anything worthwhile
   or make any meaningful impression on the world around us
   hard to credit.
And in human terms, we know that is true,
   for there is nothing special about us
   to guarantee the success of our efforts.
But we thank you that our strength lies not in ourselves but in you –
   your word,
   your love,
   your transforming power.
Time after time you have worked through those
   whom the world deemed insignificant,
   bringing the most astonishing of results
   from the most unpromising of beginnings.
Help us then to trust you now,
   and to offer our service, poor though it may seem,

confident that you will take and use it to your glory,
for your name's sake.
Amen.

Silent reflection

Reading: Mark 4:26-29

Meditation of an exhausted missionary
I thought it was down to me, the way he'd been talking.
For one awful moment
    I actually thought the dawn of the kingdom hinged on *my* efforts,
    my faithfulness,
    my contribution to the cause.
What a frightening prospect!
Imagine what it would mean, were it true:
    I'd be waiting for ever,
    looking forward in vain expectation to a day I'd never finally see,
    for, despite my best intentions, I'd be bound to fail –
    I always do –
    the job hopelessly beyond me.
Don't get me wrong,
    it's not that I haven't a role to play –
    we all have that,
    each having something valuable to contribute –
    but, thank God, his purpose is bigger than any one of us,
    his kingdom growing as often as not despite rather than because of us!
Whether we see it or whether we don't, it's there slowly growing –
    seeds starting to sprout,
    shoots bursting into flower,
    fields ripening for harvest –
    God's hand inexorably at work,
    refusing to be denied.
That doesn't excuse us, of course,
    never think that.
We all have a responsibility to help it happen,
    through word and deed to bring the kingdom closer,
    and if we fail in either we may find ourselves excluded
    when the day finally comes.
But that doesn't mean we must try and do everything,
    bear the whole burden on our shoulders,
    for we're in this together,

partners in faith,
    dependent ultimately on God to take what we offer
    and use it to his glory.
Take heart from that when progress is slow
    and your efforts seem in vain,
    when the fulfilment of his promises seems further away than ever.
Never give up,
    never lose faith,
    for the kingdom has dawned and its growth is assured –
    the final victory not down to us
    but to him.

Hymn   *O Lord of every shining constellation*
             Let all the world, in every corner, sing

Reading: Matthew 13:24-31, 36-43

Meditation of Thomas, one of the twelve disciples

Wheat and weeds,
    good and evil –
    it all sounds so simple, doesn't it –
    so straightforward;
    the distinction between them as clear as it's possible to be.
And we like to think that's true, don't we? –
    ethical issues, moral decisions,
    black and white,
    right and wrong,
    true or false?
It's so much easier that way,
    for we know precisely where we stand:
    no need to argue or debate things,
    no need even to think;
    the correct course is prescribed for us
    and woe betide anyone who dares suggest otherwise.
But is that what Jesus was saying?
I'm not so sure,
    for, look more carefully,
    and you'll see that you can't always separate the one from the other,
    not in this life, anyway.
There is good and evil, of course,
    sometimes starkly apparent,
    but the reality is that there's a bit of each in all of us,

everyone capable of rising high or falling low.
It's not for us to point the accusing finger,
    to sort out the wheat from the chaff,
    much though we'd occasionally like to.
Judge not, lest you be judged –
    isn't that what Jesus told us?
And we ignore that message at our peril,
    for we may well find ourselves in the dock
    should we pursue our case too far.
No, the advice is simple enough:
    look not to others but yourself,
    your own words,
    your own deeds,
    and ensure that the seed which was sown
    is the one that is growing.
Judgement will come in God's good time,
    our lives weighed in the balance and the harvest assessed –
    will your life prove to have been fruitful?

Silent reflection

Reading: Luke 13:6-9

Meditation of Saul, convert and apostle
What would you have done had it been you,
    had you come to that fig tree
    and found, yet again, no sign of fruit on it,
    nothing to justify the time and expense spent on its cultivation?
Would you have waited another year,
    given it one more chance to blossom despite your disappointment,
    or would you have abandoned it as a bad job,
    ordered it to be dug up to make room for a better specimen,
    one more likely to reward your investment?
Remember, this wasn't a first-year planting –
    it should have been yielding a plentiful harvest years back,
    and the likelihood is that no fruit one year means no fruit the next,
    what reason to expect any change?
Only, of course, it wasn't finally a fig tree Jesus was talking about here –
    it was you and me,
    people like us,
    and the harvest we produce in our lives,
    or, at least, the harvest we're meant to produce.

Sadly, it's all too often a different story –
    despite the care and attention God has lavished on us,
    the patient preparation and dedicated nurture,
    there's precious little to show for it,
    no harvest worthy of the name.
Why bother with us any further?
What reason to expect any sentiment from God,
    any chance to atone for past failures?
None at all.
And yet, like the gardener in the parable,
    Jesus continually pleads our cause.
One more year, he begs,
    one last opportunity for us to make amends –
    justice tempered by mercy,
    righteousness by grace.
Is there just *one* last chance?
Is that what Jesus was saying to his listeners,
    his words intended as a stern final warning?
You might have thought so, mightn't you? –
    and, yes, I suppose the day may come
    when God's patience will finally be exhausted
    and the axe has to fall.
Yet don't despair,
    for, while we shouldn't take it for granted,
    the wonderful thing is this:
    year after year Jesus goes on asking we be given one more chance,
    and year after year God continues to grant that request.

Prayer
Lord Jesus Christ,
    we know the fruits you want to see in our lives:
    love,
    joy,
    peace,
    patience,
    kindness,
    generosity,
    faithfulness,
    gentleness
    and self-control.
We know we ought to show these,
    but we know also how rarely we do,

how all too often the fruits are anything but.
Instead of living by the Spirit we live by the flesh,
    and the results are plain for all to see.
Forgive us,
    and by your grace grant us another chance to start again.
Put your Spirit within us
    and nurture our faith,
    so that the time will come when our lives will bear a rich harvest
    to the glory of your name.
Amen.

Hymn   *May the beauty of Jesus be seen in me*
             Take this moment, sign and space

Closing prayer

Loving God,
    forgive us for taking your many gifts for granted –
    forgetting, squandering and even abusing them.
Help us to rejoice in all you have given
    and to steward it wisely,
    to your glory.
Amen.

ONE WORLD WEEK

Possible visual and music material

For this service you could contact Christian Aid or any other international society for slide sets suitable for One World Week. If used in a meditative context, slides could perhaps be set to traditional music from Africa, Asia or Latin America.

Introduction

'It's a small world.' Today that seems truer than ever. We can travel across the globe in a matter of hours, watch events live by satellite from thousands of miles away, and talk to people in distant continents almost as if they are in our own front room. That fact brings enormous blessings but also new responsibilities and demands. Suddenly every person in every country has become our concern; every disaster, our disaster; everyone our neighbour. When floods strike Bangladesh, we know; when famine hits Sudan, we know; when students are massacred in Tiananmen Square, we know. Day after day, pictures of emaciated children confront us as we sit down to our meal of plenty; of the homeless as we sit in the warmth and comfort of our homes; of the poor as we enjoy an ever-rising standard of living. All these are our neighbours in today's small world. Charity may begin at home but it cannot end there. By ourselves, of course, we cannot put all the world's ills to right, nor respond to every place of need, but neither can we turn our backs and pretend that they are none of our business, for this small world is also God's world. He calls us, with his help, to reach out in his name and to make known his love in word and deed.

Hymn   *We turn to you, O God of every nation*
For the healing of the nations

Prayer

Almighty God,
   Lord of all that is,
   all that has been

and all that shall be,
we worship you.
You are sovereign over heaven and earth.
Gladly, we adore you.

Loving God,
Lord of all people,
all nations,
all cultures,
we praise you.
You are sovereign over heaven and earth.
Gladly, we adore you.

Living God,
Lord of the world,
the Church
and our lives,
we come to remind ourselves of the breadth of your love,
the extent of your purpose
and the scope of your kingdom.
You are sovereign over heaven and earth.
Gladly, we adore you.

Sovereign God,
open our minds and hearts to all you have done,
all you are doing
and all you shall yet do.
Teach us more of the fellowship we share with your people across the world,
and inspire us through their experience of your grace
and their expression of discipleship.
So may we give you the honour and glory that is rightfully yours,
this and every day.
You are sovereign over heaven and earth.
Gladly, we adore you.
In the name of Christ.
Amen.

Reading: Luke 10:25-37

Comment
The whole law encapsulated in two commandments revolving around one
word: love – it all sounds so easy, doesn't it, so wonderfully straightforward.

Or at least it does until we realise that the neighbours Jesus refers to are not just those who live next door or nearby, but everyone, everywhere; and then, suddenly, we feel overwhelmed by the scale of the challenge and the enormity of our responsibility.

Far from reducing the demands God places upon us, this summary of the law intensifies them, for instead of giving us a list of things to avoid, it challenges us to explore what we are able to do. The list is endless, for there is virtually no limit to the human need within our world. In our own society and beyond there is a multitude crying out for support and help, desperately in need of a little kindness and compassion. We cannot, of course, respond to them all, and I don't for a moment expect that Jesus intends us to, but how far do we respond to any? Our response to others must always be the acid test of our commitment; indeed, it is cited in the first letter of John as the truest yardstick of our love for God. Faith begins with God's love for us and our love for him in response, but it cannot end there, for wherever our neighbour is in need God is in need too, asking us to tend his wounds.

Meditation of the lawyer who questioned Jesus

'Teacher, ' I said, 'what must I do to inherit eternal life?'
    and I knew what he was going to say, even as I put the question.
It was typical of the man's genius,
    somehow always turning the tables on those who tried to catch him out,
    and this was to be no exception.
'What is written in the law?' he asked. 'What do you read there?'
Brilliant!
Only this time he would meet his match,
    for, unlike others, I was ready for him,
    all set to turn the tables back again and put him firmly on the spot.
So I played along, confident of emerging on top.
'Love God,' I said, 'and love your neighbour.'
It was the answer he'd been looking for,
    and he nodded with a smile of satisfaction,
    as though that was that,
    the discussion at an end,
    the issue resolved:
    'Do this and you will live.'
But that was my cue,
    and I leapt in gleefully,
    sensing the kill.
'Yes,' I smirked, 'but who is my neighbour?'
Clever, don't you think?

And I genuinely believed I had him stumped,
   one masterly stroke exposing the fatal flaw in his reasoning.
You see it sounds reasonable enough, doesn't it? –
   'Love your neighbour as yourself' –
   the sort of commandment none of us would want to argue with,
   never even presume to question.
But what does it actually mean?
If you've never asked yourself that, then it's high time you did,
   for perhaps then you'd be a little less keen on the idea,
   a little less prone to let the words trip so lightly off the tongue.
Why?
Well, quite simply, how wide do you spread the net?
How far do you go before finally drawing the line?
The people next door, are they your neighbours?
Or is it those in your street, your town, your country,
   those who share your creed, or colour, or culture?
Where does it start?
Where does it end?
You tell me.
And that's the question I put to Jesus,
   fully expecting him to flounder
   as he tried to extricate himself from my trap.
Come on, I reasoned, there had to be limits somewhere!
The Romans, for example,
   our hated oppressors –
   he couldn't mean them for a start.
Nor tax-collectors, prostitutes and sinners,
   you could write them off for certain –
   accept *them* and we'd be talking of Samaritans next, God forbid!
And how about our enemies,
   those who persecute, insult and accuse us falsely –
   don't tell me we're meant to love them too?
Preposterous!
No, I had him pinned down,
   his back to the wall,
   and there could surely be no escape?
Only then he looked at me,
   and told that unforgettable story about . . .
   you've guessed it . . . a *Samaritan*! –
   and somehow the question was once again back where it started,
   with *me*:
   'Which of these three was a neighbour to the man?'

I realised then with a stab of shock
   and a sense of disbelief,
   that he meant it,
   that he seriously wants us to treat everyone, everywhere,
   as our neighbour,
   Jew and Gentile,
   slave and free,
   male and female,
   rich and poor –
   no person outside our concern,
   no situation we can wash our hands of.
I'd put the question,
   I'd had my answer,
   and, I tell you what,
   I wish I'd never asked!

Silent reflection

Reading: Luke 16:19-31

Comment

What do we make of the parable of the rich man and Lazarus? It's not an easy passage to come to terms with, but one message leaps unmistakably from it: our responsibility to remember those less fortunate than ourselves. In this world where the divide between rich and poor is greater than ever, we need to ensure that we do not rest complacently in our plenty, giving no thought to the millions who endure hunger, disease, homelessness and exploitation. The world may have changed in many respects, but in some ways it remains depressingly the same. It is up to us to help make a difference.

Meditation of a modern-day aid worker

It could never happen now, could it?
Is that what you tell yourself
   when you read these stark and shocking words?
Nobody today could be so cruel,
   so callous as to gorge themselves senseless
   while some poor wretch lies dying of hunger on their doorstep.
The world has changed –
   more caring than it used to be;
   even the most selfish of people have some kind of conscience,
   some sense of responsibility towards others.

And yes, if we're talking of those we can see,
 those literally on our doorstep,
 perhaps you're right –
 I say, *perhaps*.
But the world has changed in other ways too;
 our neighbour is not just the one down our street,
 but across the world,
 in every country and continent.
The refugee struggling wearily to the makeshift camp in search of shelter,
 the starving child, eyes wide in mute appeal,
 the elderly couple, barely more than skin and bone,
 the broken mother, weeping over her lifeless little one –
 these are the poor man at our door,
 longing for a crumb to fall from our table.
The victim of drought,
 the family made homeless by flood,
 the people displaced by war,
 the nation oppressed by debt –
 these are the ones whose cries reach out to God
 even while our prayers fall on deaf ears.
Make no mistake,
 this was no idle tale,
 no cosy illustration of the virtue of charity.
This was Jesus laying it on the line,
 presenting the challenge fair and square,
 setting out in black and white what God requires,
 and warning us of the consequences
 should we fail to heed it.
What's that you say? 'It's not our problem.'
Of course it is,
 for there are thousands, millions, crying out for help,
 clamouring for justice,
 and while we feast on our riches,
 a multitude go hungry;
 while we thank God for his provision,
 a world asks what happened to their share.
It's time to take Jesus seriously,
 to listen to his question
 and face up to its challenge.
Are we doing enough?
Are we doing anything?
You tell me.

Hymn   *O day of God, draw near*
           Christ is the world's true light

Reading: Exodus 1:8-16

Comment

Of all the causes of division and unrest in our world, none is greater than prejudice. Despite all attempts to encourage tolerance and acceptance, prejudice runs deep in individuals and society. Race, gender, religion, age and sexuality are just some of the issues that continue to separate people one from another. We may talk of one world, but the reality is that we are as deeply divided as ever, if not more so, as witnessed by the tragic events of 11 September 2001 – a date that will be forever etched on the collective memory of humankind. In the Church there should be no place for prejudice, but let us not fool ourselves that it has no foothold in our lives. It may not be overt discrimination – though sadly that is still sometimes seen – but, as we shall explore in the following two meditations, there are other more subtle prejudices we find it hard to escape from, scarcely aware even of their existence within us. We need to recognise that danger and to ask for God's help in seeing beyond colour, culture and creed to the person underneath – a person he loved enough to send his Son to die for.

Meditation of a Hebrew slave

They hated us –
   not because we'd done wrong,
   nor through any fault on our part,
   but because we were different –
   another culture,
   another faith,
   another race.
It was as simple as that.
Immigrants, they called us – and worse;
   good for nothing layabouts, sponging off their state,
   stealing their women,
   taking their jobs,
   sapping their wealth,
   spoiling their country.
It was nonsense, of course, everybody knew it –
   we'd become part of their land,
   our lives and destiny interwoven;
   pursuing our faith, admittedly,
   worshipping our God,

but loyal, law-abiding citizens.
Oh yes, they knew,
   but they preferred to forget it,
   for they wanted someone to blame for their troubles –
   someone to hound,
   someone to hate,
   someone to hurt –
   and we were the ones chosen,
   the luckless scapegoats herded off for sacrifice.
What did they do to us? You wouldn't believe it.
Things too unspeakable, too terrible to mention!
Yet they were people, that's what I can't understand,
   ordinary people like you or me;
   folk we'd walked with, talked with,
   worked with, laughed with,
   suddenly cruel, cold, callous monsters.
One day we were human,
   the next, objects;
   one day, friend,
   the next, foe.
Who'd have believed things could change so quickly,
   the world turn upside down?
We were different, that's all,
   another tongue,
   another creed.
Yet we were people, just as they were,
   flesh and blood feeling joy and sorrow, pleasure and pain.
I thought that mattered,
   that whatever divided us, more must unite,
   but I was wrong,
   so hideously, hopelessly wrong.
Was God to blame?
I believed so at the time,
   asking myself, day after day, how he could stand by and let it happen,
   remote in heaven from such dreadful crimes on earth.
And it troubled me deeply,
   as much as the suffering itself,
   my faith shaken,
   dangling on a thread.
But it wasn't God, I realise that now –
   it was man,
   man as I never dreamt he could be;

one human being destroying another,
life counting for nothing –
and that disturbs me yet more.

Silent reflection

Reading: John 1:43-46

Meditation (to be read by two voices)
Me, prejudiced?
You must be joking!
I'm as open as the next person,
    more if anything.
The sort who takes folk as I find them,
    each to their own,
    live and let live.
All right, so maybe I do make the occasional slip-up,
    the inadvertent sexist comment;
    and perhaps I do sometimes jump to conclusions,
    swayed too much by appearances;
    but I don't mean it, you know that, Lord –
    the last thing I'd ever do is judge by the label.
Yet we have to be sensible,
    matter of fact about these things –
    it's one thing to accept,
    another to get involved;
    important to respect people,
    something else to rub shoulders with them.
After all, we're different, aren't we? –
    different backgrounds,
    different values,
    different customs,
    different everything.
So come on, Lord,
    you don't really expect me to mix with all and sundry,
    irrespective of creed or colour, do you –
    not seriously?
I'm not prejudiced –
    I'm really not –
    but they've got their lives and I've got mine,
    and quite frankly I'd rather keep it that way.

My child,
    I *am* serious, make no mistake,
    for there is more heartache caused by the barrier of prejudice
    than anything else I know of.
And though you think you're open,
    and want to be too,
    you *are* prejudiced,
    more than you'd imagine possible,
    for deep within you,
    built into the very fabric of your being,
    are innumerable preconceptions
    that shape your view of the world.
You don't do it on purpose,
    but every time you meet someone you judge them,
    by the way they dress,
    the way they talk,
    the way they think,
    the way they live;
    by the work they do,
    and the people they mix with,
    the beliefs they hold,
    and the goals they strive for.
In these and so much more your prejudice still lurks,
    unrecognised,
    unbeknown to you,
    yet colouring your attitudes,
    and fragmenting my world.
Of course people are different,
    they're meant to be,
    I made you that way on purpose –
    to help you learn,
    to stretch your minds,
    and enlarge your spirits.
And I tell you this, my child,
    when you close your lives to those around you,
    you close them also to me.

Prayer of petition and intercession

Living God,
    you have taught us through Jesus
    that our neighbours are not just those who live next door,

or those who live nearby,
   but everyone, everywhere.
And so now, once again, we pray for our world,
   our neighbours near and far.
Lord of heaven and earth,
   hear our prayer.

We pray for the victims of injustice –
   those who live in poverty,
   or face starvation,
   or have no roof over their heads.
Lord of heaven and earth,
   hear our prayer.

We pray for victims of natural disasters –
   those whose homes,
   loved ones,
   and lives have been destroyed through flood,
   earthquake or other catastrophe.
Lord of heaven and earth,
   hear our prayer.

We pray for victims of war –
   those who mourn loved ones,
   those maimed and wounded,
   and those forced to flee as refugees,
   leaving behind possessions, livelihoods
   and everything else they hold dear.
Lord of heaven and earth,
   hear our prayer.

Living God,
   teach us to respond –
   to reach out to our troubled, divided world,
   recognising the call of our neighbour in the cry of the needy;
   to see that whatever may divide us, more unites us;
   that beyond our differences lies a common humanity.
Lord of heaven and earth,
   hear our prayer.

Help us to ensure that love triumphs over hatred,
   goodness over evil,

justice over corruption,
and peace over war.
May the time come when as individuals and as nations
we live together as neighbours,
members together of an extended family of humankind,
for we ask it in the name of Christ.
Lord of heaven and earth,
hear our prayer.
In his name we ask it.
Amen.

Hymn   *God of freedom, God of justice*
Son of God, eternal Saviour

Closing prayer

Living God,
teach us that this small world is your world,
and so show us where and how in responding to others
we can respond to you,
through Jesus Christ our Lord.
Amen.

ALL SAINTS' DAY (1)

Possible visual and music material

Transparencies of Jesus and the Apostles from the slide series *Jesus of Nazareth* or *The Life of Christ* could usefully be used in this service, set to music such as the 'Pilgrims' Chorus' from *Tannhäuser* by Wagner. See Appendix (page 152).

Introduction

In 1492, as we will all no doubt have learned at school, Christopher Columbus set off from Spain in the *Santa Maria*, sailing west on a journey that he hoped would take him around the world to India. His crew were terrified, convinced that they would eventually fall off the edge of the world to their deaths. Of course, nobody fell off anywhere, and the ship eventually reached what came to be known as the West Indies. The destination may have been other than intended, but the voyage proved conclusively that the world was not flat as everyone had hitherto supposed, but round. Once done, many followed the same journey, and a thriving trade route was soon established. As so often in life, it took someone to show the way, someone to convince the doubters of what could be done.

That familiar story takes us to the heart of All Saints' Day, an occasion that celebrates those who have gone before us in faith, and whose Christian discipleship has inspired subsequent generations. It's not about holier-than-thou men and women adorned by a halo, such as we might see in a stained-glass window, but about ordinary people like you and me whose lives serve as an extraordinary example. Remember such people, take note of their way of life, and learn from them, for they have shown what can be done and what God waits to do, here and now, in your life today.

Hymn   *We come unto our father's God*
We praise, we worship you, O God

Prayer

Lord of all,
    God of space and time,
    Ruler of history,
    Sovereign over all that has been and shall be,
    we acknowledge your greatness.
O give thanks to the Lord, for he is good;
    his steadfast love endures for ever!

We gather before you,
    the God of Abraham, Isaac and Jacob,
    the God who led your people across the Red Sea
    and through the wilderness,
    who guided your chosen nation into the Promised Land,
    who spoke your word through the prophets,
    who led your people out of exile back to Jerusalem,
    and above all who lived and moved and breathed
    in the person of your Son, Jesus Christ our Lord.
O give thanks to the Lord, for he is good;
    his steadfast love endures for ever!

We praise you for your great love shown in Christ –
    for his call of twelve ordinary people to be his apostles,
    for the way you used their faith and witness to create your Church,
    and for the way across the years you have spoken
    to countless generations,
    ever more people coming to a living and saving faith in Christ.
O give thanks to the Lord, for he is good;
    his steadfast love endures for ever!

We thank you for calling us here today,
    for the fellowship of which we are a part,
    for those who have nurtured us in faith,
    and for all who have brought us encouragement and inspiration
    in our continuing journey of discipleship.
O give thanks to the Lord, for he is good;
    his steadfast love endures for ever!

We come, then, in confidence, faith, joy and thanksgiving,
    knowing that as you have guided your people across the years
    so you will continue to guide us today,
    and knowing also that in life or in death,

wherever we walk and whatever we experience,
    you will be there alongside us –
    a rock and a refuge,
    a constant source of strength,
    an unfailing giver of hope,
    an unquenchable fountain of life and love.
O give thanks to the Lord, for he is good;
    his steadfast love endures for ever!

Lord of all,
    for all who have gone before us,
    and for calling us in turn to be part of that great company of saints,
    we thank you and praise you.
O give thanks to the Lord, for he is good;
    his steadfast love endures for ever!
Thanks be to God.
Amen.

Comment

It has been observed that Jesus talked only once during his ministry about being born again but spoke several times of the need to follow him. There is an important point behind that observation, for there is a danger sometimes of making the moment of conversion all-important and forgetting that discipleship is, or should be, an unfolding journey. The Apostles followed Jesus not knowing what he was calling them to, or where their response might lead. Certainly early on he spelled out that discipleship involves cost as well as reward, but none knew exactly what the cost would be. They responded in faith, trusting that he would guide them and, apart from Judas, they kept on following even when it led to sacrifice, hostility, rejection and the death of their Master on a cross. How many of us would have followed in their place? Would we still have been there by his side after the first altercation with the Pharisees? Would we have had second thoughts when Jesus spelt out the cost of discipleship? Like the Apostles, we too may encounter moments when faith is tested and we no longer follow as we should, but Jesus will always be there, summoning us forward once again. Committing ourselves to Christ is a necessary step in discipleship, whether that involves a dramatic experience of conversion or a gradual coming to faith, but it is only a first step. Never forget that, like those who have come before us, we are involved in a continuing journey that ends only when we reach the kingdom of God in which we will be one for all eternity with all his people.

Reading: Luke 5:1-11

Meditation of Peter
He called me to follow,
    to lay down my nets and follow him.
No time to think,
    to weigh up the pros and cons;
    then and there, the need to decide.
So I did,
    on the spot –
    left everything to become one of his disciples.
And I'm glad.
No, honestly, despite everything, I'm glad,
    for I know it was the right decision,
    the only decision I could have made.
Yet if I'd known then what I know now
    it might all have been very different.
I'd have thought twice, that's for certain –
    made sure I understood the small print –
    and very likely I'd have got cold feet.
You see, I'd no real idea what I was taking on,
    even though I thought I had.
I imagined he wanted me for a few days,
    a few weeks at most,
    and then, having done my bit, I could return home,
    back to friends and family,
    back to the security of my fishing nets,
    back to the way things had always been.
But he soon put me right on that, didn't he? –
    discipleship a lifelong commitment,
    not an option you can walk away from as the mood takes you.
Well, to be honest, a few of us soon considered chucking it in,
    cutting our losses before we got in too deep.
Only we couldn't do that,
    not when it came to it,
    for we knew, though he was asking much, he was offering more.
He had the answers we were looking for,
    the words of eternal life,
    and to have walked away then
    would have been to turn our backs on our one true chance of happiness.
So we carried on,
    day after day,

week after week,
    month after month,
    following in his footsteps,
    sharing in his work.
And it was tough going, I can tell you,
    really tough –
    as a fisherman I know what I'm talking about.
Yet somehow we always found the strength we needed,
    just as he said we would,
    or at least we did until that awful last week
    when suddenly it all went wrong –
    the week Judas betrayed him, the soldiers arrested him,
    and Pilate condemned him;
    the week when we all ran for our lives,
    our love and loyalty forgotten.
It was terrible,
    more dreadful than my worst nightmares –
    I've never known fear or sorrow like I felt then –
    and I asked myself as never before,
    'Why did I ever get mixed up with Jesus?'
I still ask that sometimes, more often than you might imagine,
    for it's not got any easier following him.
There've been sacrifices to make, suffering to endure, rejection to face,
    and I know that one day, unless I'm much mistaken,
    I shall pay the ultimate price.
So yes, if I'd known then what I know now
    I might have decided differently.
It's possible – I really don't know –
    but I'm glad I didn't,
    for though it's been difficult and invariably demanding,
    it's been wonderful also;
    and I know not only was it the right decision,
    it was the best I could ever have made.

Silent reflection

Reading: Acts 7:54-60

Comment

Some years ago, a religious newspaper carried a series entitled 'What I would die for?' A variety of people were asked if there was anyone or anything for which they would be prepared to make the ultimate sacrifice, and a corresponding range of answers resulted. Some had to acknowledge there was little they would willingly die for, except perhaps their family. Others felt they would surrender their life for friends, country, freedom or faith. I like to believe I'd be among the latter should I be put to the test, ready if necessary to die for my faith, but I'm probably more like the former, the only thing for which I'd willingly face death being my family, and even then I'd have to fight my natural terror.

Life for most of us is something precious that we would not surrender lightly. The idea of sacrificing it for our principles or beliefs is one that we rightly regard with caution, especially in an age when religious extremists consider it an honour to annihilate both themselves and others in what they see as the service of God. From a Christian perspective, seeking death in this way is to belittle one of God's greatest gifts. At the same time, however, such fanaticism asks of us one important question: How far are we prepared to stand up for the things we believe in? If making a stand for convictions like personal liberty, freedom of speech and justice for all were to endanger our safety, how many of us would hide away rather than speak out? If being a Christian was made illegal and preaching the gospel a criminal offence, how many of us would quietly compromise rather than risk the consequences?

Hopefully, such questions, in this country at least, will always be academic, but for one man in the early Church the latter challenge swiftly raised its ugly head. The person in question was, of course, Stephen, the first Christian martyr. Appointed by the Apostles to share in the practical work of the Church, he swiftly made an impact through his preaching and witnessing to the gospel, but his ministry had scarcely begun when he was seized by the Jewish authorities and accused of blasphemy. It was a make-or-break moment, not just for Stephen but for the Church as a whole, his response literally a matter of life or death. Were he to back down, he might possibly save his own skin, but the gospel would be dealt a crippling blow, for others would inevitably give way in turn, and the message of the gospel would be silenced in consequence. What would you have done in Stephen's shoes? Would you have stood firm or looked for a way of escape; spoken out or kept quiet? His example asks searching questions of us all. How much does Jesus mean to us? How real is our commitment? What, if anything, are we willing to sacrifice in his service?

Meditation of Stephen

I'm too young to die,
  far, far too young!
There's still so much to live for,
  so much I want to do,

so much I've barely started.
It's not that I'm afraid of death, don't get me wrong.
It's just that I love life
    and I don't want to let it go unless I have to.
I love the sound of birds singing in the trees,
    the wind whispering through the grass,
    children laughing in the street.
I love the sight of clouds scudding across the sky,
    the sun setting across the ocean,
    the trees laden with summer fruits.
I love the feel of water fresh upon my skin,
    the smell of flowers dancing in the breeze,
    the taste of food, steaming from the oven.
I love the joy of sharing with my family,
    the pleasure of being among friends,
    the warmth of Christian fellowship –
    so much that is good which I just don't want to lose.
So why throw it away, I hear you ask me?
Why take a path that surely leads to death?
I've asked that too, believe me, countless times,
    searching for another way,
    an easier way that doesn't cost so much.
And yet although I wish there was,
    I know deep down there isn't.
I could have steered a different course – no doubt that's true –
    denied my faith or kept it under wraps.
I could have toned my message down or run away,
    not trodden on toes or taken risks.
Yet what if Christ had done the same, I ask you that –
    put safety first and not caused such a stir?
What future then would we have had?
What hope, what joy, what faith to share?
But no, he gave his all,
    despite the pain,
    despite the fear,
    despite the sorrow –
    pursuing the way of love even to the cross.
That's why I'm here now,
    jostled by the crowds,
    dragged through the streets,
    waiting for the stones to fly.
I don't want to die,

but neither did Jesus.
I'm too young to die,
   but so was he.
I want to live
   for I love life,
   passionately,
   deeply –
   but the thing is I love Jesus even more,
   just as he loved me.

Silent reflection

Hymn   *Glorious things of thee are spoken*
             O when the saints

Comment

We've thought of Stephen, who paid the ultimate price for his faith, but for others commitment brings different though, in their own way, equally challenging demands, none more so than the Apostle Paul, who endured truly astonishing privations in the cause of Christ. Yet, high though the price was, he considered it one well worth paying, for the sake of knowing and serving Christ.

Reading: 2 Corinthians 6:3-10; 2 Timothy 4:6-8

Meditation of Paul

It's been hard sometimes,
   more hard than you will ever know.
I've run the race and kept the faith,
   glad to have played my part,
   but there've been times,
   all too many times,
   when I've wondered whether I could stay the course.
It's not just been the pain, though that's been cruel enough –
   flogged,
   stoned,
   set upon and beaten.
It's not just been the exhaustion,
   though that's been crippling sometimes –
   limbs aching after yet another journey,
   mouth dry and stomach empty,
   weary to the point of death.
It's not just been the times in prison, though they've been torment –

deprived of freedom,
held in chains,
utterly alone in my cell.
They've all been costly, of course they have,
but what's been hardest to bear,
most difficult to endure,
has been the bitterness,
the sniping,
even the hatred
from those I counted my friends.
They've dogged my every step,
opposed my every move,
condemned my every success –
not merely withholding praise
but stirring up hostility,
inciting persecution,
all in the name of Christ.
It's a mystery to me, for I have given so much to make him known,
my only thought,
my only goal,
to share the faith and see his name be praised.
Was that so wrong, so false?
Yet still they thwart my work and do me down.
It's hurt me that, more than I can ever say,
and often made me question whether I can carry on.
But I have, despite it all,
and now, though you find me here in chains again,
facing trial,
facing death,
I know that I shall run the race right to the very end.
For I have learned to look to Jesus and remember all that he endured –
the pain,
the grief,
the loneliness –
all for those like me who spat upon his name.
It's been hard sometimes,
more hard than you will ever know,
but then it was hard for him too,
harder than for any of us.
Yet he saw it through faithfully, right to the very end.

Silent reflection

Comment

Faith is not always easy; indeed, there may be times when we feel unable to keep going, our strength sapped, our commitment tested and our vision battered. Whatever we may face, however, it is as nothing compared with that experienced by so many in the days of the early Church. They, too, wondered sometimes whether they could stay the course, but they were called to persevere, looking not simply to fellow Christians but above all to the example of Christ. The same is finally true for us. Remember what he has done for you, look towards the promise he has given, and so continue in what you have started, assured of the joy set before you.

Reading: Hebrews 11:32-12:2

Meditation of a writer to the Hebrews

I was ready to give up, if I'm honest,
    tired, scared, disillusioned.
We all were, every last one of us,
    just about ready to call it a day.
You ask why?
Well, you wouldn't have if you'd been there with us,
    if you'd heard the screams as we did,
    the cries for mercy,
    the gasps of agony,
    the sobs of desolation
    as yet more martyrs went to their death.
It was hard, I can tell you,
    and, worse still, we knew that at any moment our turn might come –
    the axe,
    the sword,
    the stones,
    the lions,
    all waiting for another victim to satisfy their hunger.
We'd lost hundreds,
    good honest men and women,
    honest,
    devout,
    dedicated,
    led like lambs to the slaughter,
    nothing and no one able to save them,
    not even our prayers.
What could I say to bring hope in such times?

What possible message of reassurance could I give
    when I was troubled and confused myself?
It was a crisis for me as well as them,
    every one of us struggling
    to make sense of such dreadful carnage,
    such appalling suffering,
    but there seemed nothing to say,
    no words which offered any hope or comfort.
Until suddenly I thought of Jesus,
    the pain he endured for us –
    gasping as the lash tore into his flesh,
    as the thorns pierced his head,
    as the nails smashed through his hands and feet;
    groaning as the cramps convulsed his body
    and the lifeblood seeped away.
He hadn't needed to face it,
    but he'd done so willingly,
    bearing it to the last for our sake.
And I knew then that whatever might be asked of us,
    whatever we might suffer,
    it could never be worse than the agony he endured,
    the terrible total desolation he was asked to bear.
It's not a complete answer; I can't claim that –
    it simply rephrases the question –
    but it was enough,
    for I knew then, and I could say then with confidence,
    that God is with us in our suffering,
    by our sides, whatever we might face.

Silent reflection

Prayer of intercession
Loving God,
    we remember today all who have gone ahead of us in the journey of faith,
    running the race set before them,
    and holding firm to the end.
Grant to them and to us your eternal blessing.

We remember those you called at the beginning –
    those like Abraham, Isaac and Jacob –
    examples of faith who have been an inspiration to generations since.
Grant to them and to us your eternal blessing.

We remember those you called to lead your people through adversity –
  those like Moses, Joshua, Gideon –
  examples of commitment and determination against all odds.
Grant to them and to us your eternal blessing.

We remember those you called to speak your word –
  those like Samuel, Elijah, Elisha –
  examples of wisdom and insight into your will.
Grant to them and to us your eternal blessing.

We remember those you called to rule your chosen nation –
  those like Saul, David, Solomon –
  examples of human greatness and human fallibility.
Grant to them and to us your eternal blessing.

We remember those you called to proclaim judgement and renewal –
  those like Isaiah, Ezekiel, Jeremiah –
  examples of openness to your word and courage in proclaiming it.
Grant to them and to us your eternal blessing.

We remember these and so many more leading up to the coming of Christ,
  and we remember also your servants who were a part of his ministry,
  or a part of his Church.
Grant to them and to us your eternal blessing.

We remember John the Baptist, the voice in the wilderness,
  Mary, the mother of Jesus,
  the twelve apostles, his friends and confidantes,
  the women at the empty tomb, looking in vain for his body,
  and all those countless individuals
  who were touched by his earthly ministry.
Grant to them and to us your eternal blessing.

We remember Peter, the Rock of the Church,
  Paul, apostle to the Gentiles,
  and those who have followed in their footsteps,
  saints known and unknown, near and far,
  yet each a part of the great company of your people
  in heaven and on earth.
Grant to them and to us your eternal blessing.

We remember those we have known,
    those who have been part of our own church,
    who have influenced our lives,
    who have inspired and encouraged us through their example.
Grant to them and to us your eternal blessing.

We remember those around us,
    the churches of our town,
    Christians across the country,
    fellow-believers throughout the world.
Grant to them and to us your eternal blessing.

And we pray finally for those who will succeed us,
    all who will come to faith,
    offer their service,
    and live for Christ.
Grant to them and to us your eternal blessing.

Loving God,
    we remember today all who have gone before us in the journey of faith.
Help us and all who follow to run the race as they did,
    holding firm to the end.
Grant to them and to us your eternal blessing.
Through Jesus Christ our Lord.
Amen.

Hymn   *Who would true valour see?*
              For the might of thine arm we bless you

Closing prayer
Living God,
    encourage us through those who have run the race before us,
    so that we in turn may encourage those
    who will run the race in years to come,
    until we, and they, are one with all your people,
    the great company of saints,
    in your eternal kingdom,
    world without end.
Amen.

ALL SAINTS' DAY (2)

Possible visual and music material   See suggestion for All Saints' Day (1).

Introduction   A man reviled as a collaborator with the enemy, another who almost certainly abandoned Jesus in a moment of panic, another who was to deny him despite his protestations of undying loyalty – these are just some of those whom we revere today as part of the great company of saints. They don't sound the most promising of characters, yet they, and others like them, have given inspiration and encouragement to countless generations. We focus today on the three already mentioned – Matthew, Mark and Peter – and three others – Luke, John and Paul. On one level, they were all-too-ordinary individuals, yet on another they have captured the imagination and stirred the spirit of numerous Christians subsequently walking the way of Christ. So it is we refer to them almost automatically as *Saint* Matthew, *Saint* Mark, *Saint* Luke, *Saint* John, *Saint* Peter and *Saint* Paul. They are those who, in different ways, ran their race and who offer us a lead as we run the race in turn. Through a series of meditations, we attempt in this service to recall something of their experience and to hear what they would say to us today.

Hymn   *There is a land of pure delight*
I sing a song of the saints of God

Prayer of praise
Almighty God,
   we come together as those you have called into fellowship,
   to be your people
   and to share in the rich inheritance of your saints.
I will sing of your steadfast love, O Lord, for ever.
I will proclaim your faithfulness to all generations.

We come to worship you,
>not alone,
>but as part of the world-wide family of the Church,
>united with our brothers and sisters in Christ
>across countries and continents,
>centuries and generations,
>bound together by the same Lord and the same faith.
I will sing of your steadfast love, O Lord, for ever.
I will proclaim your faithfulness to all generations.

We come as part of the great company of your people
>in heaven and on earth,
>following in the footsteps of past generations,
>picking up the torch from those who have run the race before us
>and kept the faith,
>heirs of your age-old promises.
I will sing of your steadfast love, O Lord, for ever.
I will proclaim your faithfulness to all generations.

We come as those called to build for the future,
>conscious of successive generations that will follow us,
>and mindful of our responsibility to pass on to them
>the message we have received,
>to offer them inspiration and encouragement
>through the example of our commitment.
I will sing of your steadfast love, O Lord, for ever.
I will proclaim your faithfulness to all generations.

We come, then, united with all your people of past, present, and future,
>of here, there, and everywhere,
>all those who call upon your name and offer you their service.
I will sing of your steadfast love, O Lord, for ever.
I will proclaim your faithfulness to all generations.

Remind us of that wider fellowship of which we are a part,
>and may we recognise more fully the rich heritage you have given us,
>the great cloud of witnesses to which we belong.
Open our eyes to all we may learn of you,
>through these and one another.
I will sing of your steadfast love, O Lord, for ever.
I will proclaim your faithfulness to all generations.
In the name of Christ, we pray.
Amen.

Reading: Matthew 9:9-13

Meditation of Matthew

He had time for me.
Incredible, I know, but true!
He saw beneath the surface,
    beneath the greed, the selfishness and the corruption,
    and uncovered a person I didn't even know existed.
I groaned when I saw him coming – I won't pretend otherwise;
    another self-righteous prig coming to tell me my business,
    that's what I imagined.
I'd had my fair share of those –
    well, nobody likes a tax collector, do they? –
    but we all have to earn a living somehow,
    and since the only people ready to give me a chance were the Romans,
    what could I do?
You don't seriously imagine I enjoyed working for them, do you,
    but someone had to do it, so why not me?
I suppose Jesus understood that, for *he* didn't criticise or condemn –
    none of the two-faced hypocrisy of the Pharisees,
    the usual accusing glances or obscene gestures –
    just those two lovely words:
    'Follow me.'
You could have knocked me over,
    for it was the last thing I expected,
    took the wind right out of my sails.
But, more important, I was excited,
    moved,
    fascinated,
    because he had time for me.
He hadn't written me off,
    he hadn't seen only the outside.
He accepted me as I was,
    with all my sin sticking to me.
And the funny thing was, once he did that
    it was me who pointed to my faults,
    not him.
I felt ashamed,
    painfully aware of all that was wrong,
    longing to be different;
    yet at the same time set free,

forgiven,
   offered a new beginning.
I followed, of course –
   what else could I do?
Would you refuse a man like that?
Well, perhaps you would, but I'm glad I didn't,
   because despite everything since –
   the times I've let him down,
   the occasions I've misunderstood,
   the mistakes I've made,
   the faults I still have –
   he goes on accepting me day after day,
   not for what I might become
   but for what I am!

Silent reflection

Reading: Mark 14:51-52

Meditation of Mark

Was that really me, all those years ago,
   running naked from the garden?
I've heard the story so many times,
   how they'd been with Jesus sharing the Last Supper,
   how they broke bread and drank wine,
   how they followed him into the garden, and fell asleep,
   how Judas betrayed him with a kiss.
Yes, I'd heard it all, and shed tears with the best of them.
But it's that young man who always fascinated me –
   the one they so nearly collared,
   so nearly dragged with Jesus before Caiaphas –
   because *that* was *me!*
I'd been there all evening, hoping to catch sight of the Master,
   hiding quietly in the bushes,
   and when he came out, my heart leapt.
He was there, alone,
   just a few yards away,
   the rest of his disciples waiting at a distance,
   and he so near I could almost touch him,
   so close I could hear his every word.

But delight turned to horror as the soldiers arrived,
  dark figures silhouetted against the flames of their torches,
  like demons emerging out of hell.
I was paralysed with fear,
  realising I too was in danger,
  and eventually it was too much for me.
I broke cover and ran for it –
  heard the shouts,
  felt their hands grasp my clothing,
  but kept on running, desperate to get away.
And somehow I made it,
  running naked and tearful into my mother's arms.
It's a long time ago now, of course,
  many years,
  yet do you know what?
Nobody knows that boy was me.
It's been my guilty secret all this while,
  my skeleton in the cupboard,
  the ghost that I've never had the courage to exorcise.
I should have told them, had done with it like Peter did,
  but *he* had no choice, did he?
That's the difference – they knew about *him*,
  he couldn't hide.
My failure was unknown to anyone but me,
  and as time went by I decided to keep it that way.
It became harder to tell,
  harder to face,
  and so much easier to keep locked away.
Yet it's *not* been easy, not really,
  for it's always there,
  my secret shame,
  my private pain.
They trust me now, that's the trouble,
  respect me,
  look to me for guidance and leadership,
  but I can't help asking myself,
  'What if they knew? What then?'
Yet Jesus knows,
  and he's accepted me all this time.
It's no good: I have to tell them,
  for until I'm honest with others I'm not being honest with him
  or myself.

Reading: Luke 1:1-4

Meditation of Luke

I never knew him myself,
   not in the way the others did.
And yet I felt I had, such was the way Peter talked about him.
He was obviously quite a person, Jesus; that much is clear.
You can't make that sort of impression without being a bit special.
We used to sit, Peter and I, talking deep into the night,
   and as he spoke his face would come alive with pleasure.
He had so many memories –
   the day Jesus first called him, right out of the blue,
   the way he healed the sick,
   cured the insane,
   fed the multitude,
   stilled the storm.
And then, of course, that final meal,
   the scene in the garden,
   the agony on the cross,
   the empty tomb –
   so much to share, good and bad.
I was spellbound,
   completely hooked.
It wasn't just what Peter said
   but the way he said it.
He meant every word!
It was real for him,
   vital,
   as much good news after all that time
   as when it had first happened.
Not that he pulled any punches –
   there was no glossing over the awkward episodes,
   no pretending it had all been easy.
He told me how he'd recognised Jesus was the Messiah,
   but also how he'd failed to understand what that meant;
   about the moment on the mountaintop,
   but also when the cock crowed;
   about the time he'd knelt at Jesus' feet,
   but refused to let Jesus kneel at his.
He knew he wasn't perfect,
   realised full well he still had much to learn,
   but he'd been changed for all that;

through Jesus become a new man.
I wish I could have known Jesus like he did,
   heard him, seen him, met him for myself.
But like I say, I never did.
Yet I do know him,
   personally,
   as my closest friend,
   and not just through what Peter said.
That was important, of course it was;
   it started there –
   my interest captured,
   my imagination aroused –
   but I've moved on since then,
I can't fully explain it,
   and it probably sounds crazy,
   but I feel him with me day by day, always by my side,
   I hear his voice, see his hand and experience his presence;
   and I honestly feel that though I never knew him in the flesh,
   I know him as well as Peter,
   as well as anyone could ever do,
   here,
   alive,
   in my heart!

Silent reflection

Hymn   *Sing we the King who is coming to reign*
              Christ is made the sure foundation

Reading: John 1:1-18

Meditation of John, Disciple of Jesus

There's only one word for it,
   one word that gets anywhere near the truth,
   that sums up the wonder of it all,
   and that's 'Jesus'.
Trust me, I know,
   for I've spent a lifetime trying to find the right words.
Since I followed Jesus all those years ago,
   since I sat with the apostles in that upper room,
   since we went out teaching and preaching in the Master's name,
   I've been looking for ways in which to describe my experience,

and I've used words,
   masses of them,
   more than I can begin to count.
When I stood and preached to the multitudes,
   when I nurtured believers in their new-found faith,
   when I prayed for the sick,
   led times of worship,
   reminisced with friends,
   witnessed to strangers,
   words, words, words . . .
   but they've never been sufficient,
   never begun to express what I really want to say.
And now more than ever I find that's true,
   as I try to record the good news of Jesus Christ.
I've written so much,
   page after page,
   my own words and his,
   woven together as best I can into a tapestry of his life.
I've told of beginnings and endings,
   of his signs, teaching and actions.
I've spoken of those lesser-known characters,
   the ones Matthew, Mark and Luke missed out,
   and I've given details of those private moments,
   when it was just us and Jesus together as the end drew near.
I've tried,
   I've really tried to get it across,
   to tell you what Jesus meant to me and to so many others,
   but there's so much more I could still write,
   so much I've had to leave out.
I could go on to the end of time
   and still not do justice to all I want to tell you.
That's why I say there's only one word,
   one word that says it all,
   because Jesus was the fulfilment,
   the embodiment,
   the personification of God's *living* word.
The Law and the Prophets foretold him,
   the universe in all its glory proclaims him,
   and if you want to listen,
   if you want to hear,
   if you want to understand what life is all about,
   then take my word for it,

the only way is to know him for yourself:
the word made flesh!

Silent reflection

Reading: John 21:15-19

Meditation of Peter

Three times he asked me,
    three times the same simple yet searching question:
    'Do you love me, Peter?'
And I was getting fed up with it,
    not to say a little hurt.
After all, he should have known by then, surely.
I'd followed him for three years,
    and I thought we'd become close –
    he gave that impression, anyway.
The 'Rock', he'd called me,
    the one on whom he'd build his Church –
    an expression of trust, if ever there was one –
    so how could he doubt me now,
    let alone question my love?
But then, of course, I remembered that bold, brash promise of mine:
    'Though all become deserters because of you, I will never desert you' –
    and suddenly I understood.
He'd known I would fail, even then,
    not only abandon but deny him,
    and he knew too how sick I'd felt,
    how wretched and ashamed
    when the knowledge of my failure finally sunk home.
But there was no anger from him,
    no recriminations,
    no rebuke.
His concern was for me, not himself,
    his sole desire to wipe the slate clean and start again,
    and this was my chance to deal with the guilt,
    to exorcise the demon once and for all.
Three times I'd denied him,
    three times he put the question,
    and at last I could put the record straight,
    declare to him what I should have declared to others:
    'Yes, Lord; you know that I love you.'

We couldn't change the past, we both knew that,
    but with his help we could put it behind us and change the future,
    and that's what he offered me that day,
    a new beginning,
    a fresh chapter,
    life dawning for me as surely as it had dawned again for him.
I was restored,
    cleansed,
    forgiven,
    the ghost finally laid to rest,
    and I owed it all to him,
    the man whom I abandoned so freely,
    yet who refused to abandon me!

Silent reflection

Reading: 2 Corinthians 12:7b-10

Meditation of Paul

I could think about nothing else at the time but that affliction of mine,
    that thorn in the flesh, as I finally came to call it.
It dominated my whole life, and very nearly destroyed me,
    sapping my strength,
    destroying my confidence,
    eating into the very fabric of my faith.
Try as I might, I just couldn't get it out of my head –
    it was always there,
    preying on my mind,
    lurking in the shadows,
    waiting to devour me.
When I woke up in the morning it was waiting to meet me,
    a constant reminder of my weakness.
When I walked in the street it pursued me,
    striking me down when I least expected.
When I talked with friends it was there too,
    breaking into our conversation,
When I turned to God in prayer even there it turned up,
    insinuating itself between us.
And I was getting desperate,
    sucked ever deeper into a dark pit of despair,
    the laughter, the love, the life being drained from me.
Why? – I asked.

Why me?
What sin had I committed?
What penance did I have to do
    before God would have pity and set me free?
I'd make it worth it, I told him,
    not just for me but both our sakes.
I could do so much more,
    serve him so much better,
    if only he'd hear my prayer.
But there was no answer,
    no release,
    nothing.
I begged him again,
    angry,
    disappointed,
    resentful.
But it made no difference –
    still nothing.
So I left off for a while,
    until my patience could take it no longer,
    the frustration too much to bear.
And then once more I asked,
    grovelling this time,
    begging,
    pleading.
But yet again, nothing,
    just a blank, empty silence.
Or so I thought,
    until suddenly this picture of Jesus came to me,
    his eyes filled with pain,
    his body broken,
    and on his head a crown of thorns;
    the blood trickling down his tortured face,
    the hands outstretched in agony –
    and all at once I knew I was wrong.
He'd heard me, all right,
    and answered,
    only I hadn't been ready to listen.
For it was there, in the sorrow and suffering of the Cross,
    that God fulfilled his eternal purpose;
    there, in what the world counts weakness,
    that God showed us true greatness!

So have I finally come to terms with this problem of mine,
   exorcised the demon that's haunted me for so long?
No, I can't claim that,
   for I still have my moments,
   still sometimes ask why,
   and still hope some day it might be different.
But when I catch myself feeling like that I stop and think of Jesus,
   and I realise again that in my weakness is God's strength.

Silent reflection

Comment

Just six of the saints of God – celebrated, revered individuals who ran the race and kept the faith, yet who, as we have seen, were ordinary people with the same weaknesses, frailties and foibles as you and me. You, too, are called into the company of God's people, one of his chosen saints. You may not feel like it, you may feel anything but, yet God has called you, as you are, to journey in faith, following in the footsteps of those who have gone before, and serving as an example to those who will come after you. Looking to the great crowd of witnesses set before us, let us run *our* race with perseverance.

Prayer of intercession

Sovereign God,
   we have thought of the wider fellowship that we share in Christ,
   the great company of your people in heaven and on earth
   to which we are privileged to belong,
   and so now we pray for those
   who seek, in turn, to follow you today.
Rock of ages,
   hear our prayer.

We pray for those for whom commitment is costly –
   those who face hostility, discrimination,
   repression and persecution
   for the sake of the gospel.
Give them strength and courage,
   so that they may keep the faith.
Rock of ages,
   hear our prayer.

We pray for those who are finding the journey of discipleship difficult –
   troubled by doubts,

plagued by temptation,
   or simply slipping back into old ways.
Give them support and reassurance,
   so that they may walk with new confidence.
Rock of ages,
   hear our prayer.

We pray for those expressing their faith in action –
   individuals and agencies working, often against the odds,
   to give expression to the love of Christ.
Give them love and compassion,
   so that they may make Christ real for others.
Rock of ages,
   hear our prayer.

We pray for all seeking to communicate their faith –
   ministers, evangelists, missionaries, chaplains,
   but also ordinary, everyday believers like us –
   each telling in their own way what Jesus means to them.
Give them wisdom and inspiration,
   so that they may speak your word with power.
Rock of ages,
   hear our prayer.

Sovereign God,
   we pray for Christians everywhere
   striving to live out their faith in the world of today
   with all the pressures, challenges and demands that confront them.
Give them guidance and encouragement
   so that they may grow in grace.
Grant them humility to learn more of you each day
   and the ability to share their experience
   simply and effectively with others,
   making Christ known through word and deed.
Rock of ages,
   hear our prayer.
All this we ask through Jesus Christ our Lord.
Amen.

Hymn   *For all the saints*
           Jesus shall reign where'er the sun

Closing prayer

Lord Jesus Christ,
    the same yesterday, today and for ever,
    with all your people in every age,
    we give you praise and glory,
    this day and for evermore.
Amen.

Remembrance Sunday (1)

Possible visual and music material   Numerous slides depicting scenes from the two world wars have been produced, but I am not sure whether any of these are available commercially. If you are able to get hold of some, they would make a powerful impact set to music such as Edward Elgar's 'Nimrod' from the *Enigma Variations* or the slow movement of his First Symphony. An ideal place for them would be after the first meditation.

Introduction   Today, like several days in the month of November, is a day for remembering, for looking back and recognising all that we owe to so many. It is a day also for acknowledging the price paid for the peace and freedom we enjoy in the present, and for considering the future, praying for and committing ourselves, so far as we are able, to preserving those gifts for future generations. Come, then, with your eyes open to all that has been and shall be, and commit all to the God who holds past, present and future in his hands.

Hymn   *Lead me from death to life* (metrical version of World Peace Prayer)
'I have a dream,' a man once said

Prayer of praise

Sovereign God,
   we praise you today for the freedom we enjoy
   as a nation and as individuals –
   freedom of speech and expression,
   freedom from war and oppression –
   a freedom secured at such enormous human cost.
For all we owe to so many,
   receive our thanks.

We praise you for those who made such freedom possible,
   the countless thousands who sacrificed life and limb in two world wars
   and in subsequent conflicts,
   leaving homes and loved ones often to return no more.
For all we owe to so many,
   receive our thanks.

We praise you for all who have fought against tyranny, hatred and evil,
  prepared to sacrifice everything
  rather than allow such forces to hold sway,
  and we salute their courage shown in the face of danger,
  their dedication to duty,
  their determination to battle on against all odds.
For all we owe to so many,
  receive our thanks.

We praise you for the peace we enjoy today –
  a peace which we need to treasure constantly,
  nurture carefully
  and safeguard always,
  recognising the price at which it was won.
For all we owe to so many,
  receive our thanks.

We praise you for those today who safeguard
  international freedom and justice –
  members of UN peace-keeping forces in places of continuing tension,
  striving to maintain democracy,
  to keep rival factions apart,
  to protect innocent civilians
  and to ensure a lasting end to hostilities.
For all we owe to so many,
  receive our thanks.

Sovereign God,
  we praise you today for the freedom we enjoy,
  and we pray that the day will come when there will be no more war,
  when the nations of our world will live in harmony,
  and when you will rule over all.
Until that time, help us to learn the lessons of the past,
  to remember its sacrifices,
  and to work as far as we are able for peace.
For all we owe to so many,
  receive our thanks.
Through Jesus Christ our Lord.
Amen.

Comment

Why remember events that happened many years ago? Why perpetuate
memories of a conflict long since past? Many today understandably raise

such questions and, had we enjoyed unbroken global peace since the two world wars, their arguments would carry much force. Only, of course, the reality is that conflict continues to be all too common. Central America, the Falklands, Bosnia, Northern Ireland, the Middle East and the attack on the World Trade Centre, to name but a few, have all given stark reminders of the tensions that continue to scar our world. There are no easy answers to such divisions, and history has taught us that peace, if secured at all, is a fragile thing, hard won and easily broken. Yet the cost of war reminds us of the need to establish global justice and to break down the barriers that continue to exact such a heavy toll. We owe it not just to the countless human victims of war but, above all, to God – the greatest victim of all.

Meditation: I was there

I was there –
    there in the trenches among the rats and lice,
    struggling in the mud
    as the machine guns spewed out their hail of bullets,
    lying in agony beside the rows of corpses,
    all around me the bodies of my friends,
    limb torn from limb,
    wounds gaping,
    bodies shattered beyond recognition –
    and my heart bled with them.

I was there in the city as the bombs cascaded from the sky,
    there among the screams and sobs,
    beating back the flames,
    pulling away the rubble,
    searching frantically with the mother for the little one
    she would never see again –
    and, like her, my heart went cold with horror.

I was there in the prison camp,
    beaten, starved, tortured,
    watching helplessly as one by one my loved ones were led away,
    as the smoke rose above the ovens,
    as the carts trundled from the gas chamber, laden with death –
    and my heart groaned in despair.

I was there as the missile struck and the world disintegrated,
    as the deadly cloud rose high above the devastation,
    as we retched in agony,

as we coughed up blood,
as we sat hopelessly in the cancer ward, knowing the end was near –
and my heart cried out in anger.

Yes, I was there,
the one who died on a cross to put an end to death and misery,
dying again,
and again,
and if you think it broke your heart,
remember this:
it broke mine too.
You can't change what's been,
but you can what's yet to be,
and, believe me, you would if you'd seen what I've seen.

I was there,
and I'm begging you,
please,
please,
PLEASE,
don't let it happen again!

Silent reflection

Reading: John 15:13

Two minutes' silence

Sentences
They shall not grow old, as we that are left grow old.
Age shall not weary them, nor the years condemn.
At the going down of the sun and in the morning we will remember them.
We will remember them.

Reading: Psalm 46:1-3

Hymn   *Make me a channel of your peace*
             Let there be peace on earth

Comment
Every night, in the town of Ypres in Belgium, a crowd gathers at 8 o'clock
beneath the Menin Gate to observe the ceremony of the Last Post. It is a

simple yet profoundly moving tribute to all those who gave their lives during the First World War. The location could hardly be more fitting, this beautiful town having been reduced to rubble during that conflict but lovingly restored afterwards, stone for stone. More powerful still, on the Menin Gate are inscribed the names of the thousands of soldiers killed in the Ypres-Salient and with no known grave. There can surely be few more graphic reminders of the awful cost of war. The following poem seeks to bring home that cost and to prompt reflection on our responsibility today to work for peace. It was written during my time with Toc H, a national movement committed to breaking down barriers of prejudice and discrimination in society, and it encapsulates the principles at the heart of that movement: building bravely, loving widely, thinking fairly and witnessing humbly.

Meditation: It was March

It was March when we visited Ypres,
  just a few weeks short of the spring,
  the flowers were starting to open,
  the birds beginning to sing.
Outside, in fertile lowlands,
  the grass grew lush and green,
  no sign now of the carnage
  which once these fields had seen.
And in the busy centre,
  a constant hum of sound,
  as a milling throng of people
  pursued their daily round.
Few hints here of the horrors
  that racked this charming place,
  mock medieval splendour
  and pleasant open space.

But as the sunlight faded
  and night began to fall,
  a little crowd assembled
  beside the city wall.
In different moods they stood there,
  some laughing, some in tears,
  some talking of the weather,
  some hiding inner fears.
But all at once fell silent
  as the clock came round to eight,

and a poignant tribute sounded
   beneath the Menin Gate.
Another sad reminder,
   another fond farewell;
   a proud and thankful blessing,
   a heart-rending death knell.

And as the bugles faded
   till their sound was heard no more,
   we saw then all too clearly
   the dreadful face of war.
Instead of names around us
   there were young men in their prime,
   a tragic generation
   cut down before their time.
Our hearts were there beside them,
   we stood knee-deep in mud,
   and shared the awful horror
   of fields dyed red with blood.
We heard their cries of anguish,
   we felt their searing pain,
   and we understood more clearly
   this must never be again.

Yet the battle is not over,
   though the war may long be past,
   the fighting may have halted
   but the cause is only masked.
Unless we come together,
   until we learn to share;
   until we love more widely
   and think in ways more fair;
   until we build so bravely
   that all we say and do
   gives our hope of breaking barriers
   some hope of coming true,
   then the Last Post may be sounded
   in the future just the same,
   but the thousands who it heralds
   will all have died in vain.

Silent reflection

Prayer of intercession

Living God,
    we are here to remember –
    to remember again the awful cost of war,
    to remember the millions who gave their lives
    for the cause of freedom,
    to remember the courage and heroism, fear and pain,
    tragedy and grief that touched so many.
At the going down of the sun, and in the morning,
    we will remember them.

Living God,
    we are here to remember all of this,
    and much more besides –
    those who still mourn the loved ones they lost,
    those whose lives even now are blighted by war,
    those scarred in body, mind or spirit,
    those for whom warfare has meant life can never be the same again.
At the going down of the sun, and in the morning,
    we will remember them.

And we remember also those who strive to establish and maintain peace –
    governments and world leaders,
    United Nations forces and diplomats,
    pressure groups and ordinary people;
    all who in different ways strive to promote harmony between nations,
    giving victims of war the opportunity to live a normal life once more.
At the going down of the sun, and in the morning,
    we will remember them.

Living God,
    we remember today the cost of war,
    and the price of peace.
Help us to go on remembering, tomorrow and every day,
    and to do all in our power to work for your kingdom,
    here on earth.
At the going down of the sun, and in the morning,
    we will remember them.
In the name of Christ we pray.
Amen.

Reading: Isaiah 11:1-9

Comment

A vision of the future or sentimental nonsense; a realistic picture of what life might be like or a wistful portrait of what it might have been – what do you make of the words of Isaiah chapter 11? Memorable words they certainly are, but are they simply poetic imagery or prophetic foresight? In terms of this life at least, both those appraisals contain an element of truth. In recent years we have seen startling moves towards peace in some quarters of the world, yet also there have been unspeakable atrocities and mind-boggling inhumanity. Sadly, for every reason to hope there seems to be still more cause to despair, and, eventually, few of us can avoid disillusionment setting in. We'd like to believe in a world such as the prophet paints – a time of peace and harmony, when violence, discord and hatred will be a thing of the past – but most of us take such claims with a strong pinch of salt. Life, we tell ourselves, is just not like that. Realism rather than the idealism invariably wins the day. Such an attitude is understandable given the lamentable record of human history and the continuing divisions in our world today, yet it cannot finally be acceptable. *We* may abandon the world to its fate – God never will. He will not rest until his will is done and his kingdom established, on earth as it is in heaven. It may seem light years away from the world as we know it today, but we must never lose that vision of what life can become, nor stop working towards it.

Meditation of Isaiah

Does this sound daft to you –
   a wolf lying down with a lamb,
   a lion grazing with an ox,
   a child playing happily with a snake?
It does to me, I have to admit it,
   now I've had time to consider the implications.
But it didn't at the time,
   not when the idea first caught hold of me.
You see, I had this picture of a different kind of world,
   a society where barriers are broken down,
   where all the petty disputes that so often divide us
   are a thing of the past.
Imagine it –
   no more violence,
   no more fear,
   no more hatred,
   no more suffering;
   a world at one with itself,

all creatures living together in harmony,
nation existing peaceably alongside nation,
people set free to be themselves –
valued,
loved,
respected,
not for what we can get out of them,
but simply for what they are.
Is that so daft?
Well, yes, it probably is,
because nine times out of ten,
ninety-nine times out of a hundred,
for most of us, when the pressure's on,
it's number one who comes first,
a question of 'I'm all right and never mind the rest'.
We'd like it to be different, obviously,
but even when we're not simply paying lip-service to high ideals,
we can't finally change ourselves, try as we might.
Yet give me one thing –
it's an incredible idea, isn't it –
this world of peace and justice?–
a beautiful picture –
worth striving for, I'd say,
even worth dying for.
And who knows, one day,
just maybe,
somebody might actually come along
with the faith and courage not just to dream about it,
but to bring it about;
not simply to share the vision,
but to live in such a way that it becomes real –
God's kingdom, here on earth.

Silent reflection

Prayer of petition
Almighty God,
on this day of remembering,
help us to learn the lessons of the past:
to understand the cost of war,
the price of peace,
the scope of human depravity

and the extent of human self-sacrifice.
Help us to learn those lessons –
    to live and work for peace,
    to stand up against evil,
    to serve and not to count the cost,
    to work in whatever way we can for a better world.
Forgive us that we do not remember as often as we should,
    forgetting how fortunate we are to live in freedom
    and how lucky to enjoy peace;
    forgetting those who still suffer from the wounds of battle
    and others who even now mourn their loved ones.
Speak to us today
    and help us not only to say the words but truly to mean them:
    'We will remember them.'
Amen.

Hymn   *Put peace into each other's hands*
                Your kingdom come, O God

Closing prayer

Living God,
    teach us to remember the lessons of the past,
    so that we may better appreciate the present
    and work always for a better future,
    in the name of Christ.
Amen.

REMEMBRANCE SUNDAY (2)

Possible visual and music material   See Remembrance Sunday (1)

Introduction   Remembering isn't always easy, is it? We can remember some things with no difficulty, but we forget many others, and all too often they seem to be the things we need to remember most! So it is that some of us resort to such props as a knot in a hankie or a memo-board in the kitchen, in the hope that these may jog our memory.

Such, increasingly, is the rationale behind Remembrance Day. Every year, the number of those who lived through one or both of the two World Wars diminishes, yet for that reason the occasion becomes more rather than less important. We have only to witness the horrors of Bosnia, or the continuing violence in the Middle East and so many other parts of the world, to realise that things haven't changed as much as we might like to think. Disturbingly, some today dare to suggest that horrors like the Holocaust or 'ethnic cleansing' never actually happened, thus dismissing, at a stroke, the suffering, terror and anguish experienced by so many millions. The fact is that we cannot afford to forget the past. Remembrance Day does not glorify war but rather recalls the price of peace, reminding us of the evil and inhumanity that people can stoop to, and the sacrifice so many made to ensure that such tyranny did not triumph. It purposely thrusts such things back into our consciousness – lest we forget.

Hymn   *Behold, the mountain of the Lord*
God is our strength and refuge

Prayer

Almighty God,
  we come today to remember all you have done –
  your creative acts,

your mighty deeds throughout history,
your dealings with your people,
your gift of Christ,
your love experienced daily in our lives.
Remind us of all we owe,
lest we forget.

We remember those who lost their lives
in the two world wars and later conflicts –
the horror they endured,
the determination they displayed,
the courage they showed and the sacrifices they made
to defend the values we continue to hold dear today,
and to ensure lasting peace.
Remind us of all we owe,
lest we forget.

Forgive us that so often and so easily we do forget.
We fail to recognise all you have done for us,
to remember all we have received,
to count our many blessings,
or to appreciate how much we owe to you and so many.
Remind us of all we owe,
lest we forget.

Almighty God,
through all things you remember us –
help us to remember you!
Remind us of all we owe,
lest we forget.
We ask it in the name of Christ.
Amen.

Reading: Deuteronomy 7:18; 8:2

Comment

It is hard for us to imagine the full horror of what so many have been through in war, but it is vital that we try, for only then can we appreciate all we owe to the millions we remember today, and so understand the importance of maintaining peace for future generations. The following meditation, written during a visit to the war graves of Flanders, asks how it must have felt to be one of the countless young soldiers sent out to the battlefields of 'The Great War'.

Meditation

How did you feel that morning
  when the call-up papers came through?
Did your blood run cold, or excitement take hold
  at the thought that your country needs you?

How did you feel that morning
  when the time came to set off from home?
Did you conquer your fears, or break down in tears
  with the loved ones you'd soon leave alone?

How did you feel that morning
  when you first set foot in the trench?
Did you brush it aside, or wish you could hide
  from the horror, the carnage, the stench?

How did you feel that morning
  when your friend was blown up by a shell?
Did you rush to his aid, or just stand there, afraid
  that you'd somehow been whisked off to hell?

How did you feel that morning
  when they sent you over the top?
Did you shout with relief, or in sheer disbelief,
  vainly pray that the nightmare would stop?

How did you feel that morning
  when the bullets started to fly?
Did you think even then you might cheat death again
  or did you know you were going to die?

How did you feel that morning
  as the lifeblood slipped slowly away?
Did you try to make sense of these crazy events
  or with one final breath try to pray?

How do I feel this morning
  in the face of such slaughter and sorrow?
Do I just stand aghast as I think of the past
  or give all for a better tomorrow?

Silent reflection

Comment

Reminded of all who paid the highest price and all to whom we owe our freedom, let us remember in silence those who have died in war, and let us pray that the peace they won for us need never again be broken.

Two minutes' silence

Sentences

They shall not grow old, as we that are left grow old.
Age shall not weary them, nor the years condemn.
At the going down of the sun and in the morning we will remember them.
We will remember them.

Prayer of petition

Loving God,
   once more we have been reminded of the terrible cost of war,
   the suffering and sacrifice of so many,
   the depths of inhumanity some have sunk to,
   and the heights others have climbed in the service of others.
Teach us to remember,
   not just today but always.

We have heard again today
   words that have been spoken so many times over the years,
   words in which we promise never to forget.
Yet the tragedy is we do forget, all too easily –
   this annual remembrance a token gesture,
   observed sincerely and respectfully
   but then over and done with for another year.
Teach us to remember,
   not just today but always.

We forget how fortunate we are to live in freedom,
   how lucky we are to enjoy peace.
We forget how some still suffer from the wounds of battle,
   and others even now mourn their loved ones.
Teach us to remember,
   not just today but always.

Loving God,
    forgive us that, despite our words and best intentions,
    we have so often forgotten the lessons of the past.
Speak to us through all we have heard and shared today,
    so that we can truly say,
    and truly mean,
    'We will remember them.'
Teach us to remember,
    not just today but always.
For we ask it in the name of Christ our Lord.
Amen.

Hymn   *For the healing of the nations*
              Christ is the world's true light

Comment

For over fifty years in Britain we have enjoyed peace. There have, of course, been confrontations involving British forces – in the Falklands, the Gulf War, Kosovo, Afghanistan – but civilians at home have been largely untouched by the fighting. There is a danger that we might come to take peace for granted, forgetting the price at which it was won, and the ease with which it could be lost. The following meditation reminds us of the need to celebrate peace whilst also remembering the cost of war.

Meditation

There were crowds in the streets of London the day the peace was signed,
    they sang in exultation; they danced, they wined, they dined;
    for the dreadful war was over, the slaughter at an end,
    and now at last a broken world could slowly start to mend.
But among the celebrations, the thankful, happy cries,
    a multitude were weeping, no laughter in their eyes.
For these there was no reason to share the festive mood,
    their hearts were bowed with sorrow, their every thought subdued.
For while the throng around them gave vent to shouts of joy,
    they grieved a loving husband, they mourned their precious boy,
    they thought of dads or brothers, of cousins, nephews too,
    of uncles, colleagues, trusted friends, so many they once knew.

So when some talk of glory, of mighty deeds once done,
    think also of the suffering with which it all was won.
And when they speak of victory upon that glorious day

remember all those buried in fields so far away.
It's true that time's a healer, the war now long ago,
    it's true we've learned to live with the ones we once called foe;
    but many still are haunted by thoughts of those they lost,
    still struggling with their feelings, still counting out the cost.
So if you would pay tribute and honour those who fell,
    then work for peace and justice, and make your freedom tell.
There is no way more fitting we can repay the debt,
    nor better way of saying that we will not forget.

Silent reflection

Reading: Revelation 21:1-4; 22:5

Comment

The Apostle John in those words looks forward to a time when there will be no more war, suffering or sorrow. Few of us can fail to be moved by that vision, but can it only be fulfilled in the world to come, beyond the prejudices, division, sin and selfishness of the world as we know it? Almost certainly the answer is yes, but that does not mean we can give up on the present, reconciled to further conflict and warfare. We need to pray and work for peace in whatever ways we can, recognising that it begins with us and our relationships, and recognising also, though it may not always seem like it, that God is at work despite all that conspires against him, striving to build his kingdom and fulfil his purpose, here and now.

Meditation of John

I had a dream last night,
    a wonderful, astonishing dream –
    so real,
    so vivid,
    that it will live with me for the rest of my days.
I caught a glimpse of God,
    enthroned in majesty,
    encircled by the great company of heaven,
    and there at his right hand,
    exalted,
    lifted up in splendour,
    our Lord Jesus Christ,
    King of kings
    and Lord of lords!

It was wonderful,
   breathtaking,
   indescribable.
Yet I have to share it with you somehow –
   clutching at metaphors,
   searching for the right words,
   but at least giving you some idea of what I saw.
Why? I hear you say.
What does it matter if it was only a dream?
And I take your point, believe me.
Yet I have this feeling, deep within,
   no – more than just a feeling – this certainty,
   that God was speaking to me through that dream;
   speaking to *me*,
   to *you*,
   to everyone with ears to hear and a mind to listen.
He was telling us that in the chaos of this humdrum world,
   the changes and chances of this uncertain life;
   despite all the pain, suffering, evil and sorrow,
   everything that seems to fight against him,
   God is there,
   working out his purpose,
   slowly but surely.
And one day,
   in the fullness of time,
   his kingdom shall come
   and his will be done.
Don't ask me when, for I can't tell you that,
   but though we may not see it
   and though we may not feel it,
   I am assured that he will triumph.
Joy will take the place of sorrow.
Life will follow death.
Love will be victorious!

Silent reflection

Prayer of intercession
Lord of all,
   hear us now as we pray for the victims of war
   and for peace in our world.

We pray for those across the world who bear the scars of conflict –
    the injured, maimed and mentally distressed,
    those who have lost their limbs, their reason or their loved ones
    through the horrors of war.
Lord, in your mercy,
    hear our prayer.

We pray for those left homeless or as refugees,
    those who have lost their livelihoods and security,
    and those who still live in daily fear for their lives.
Lord, in your mercy,
    hear our prayer.

We pray for children who have been orphaned,
    parents who mourn their children,
    husbands and wives who have lost their partners –
    countless families whose lives will never be the same again.
Lord, in your mercy,
    hear our prayer.

We pray for those in the armed forces,
    charged with keeping the peace in countries across the world –
    their work involving months away from family and friends,
    and often danger to themselves.
Lord, in your mercy,
    hear our prayer.

We pray for world leaders and rulers,
    politicians and diplomats –
    those whose decisions and negotiations affect the lives of so many
    and in whose hands peace has been entrusted.
Lord, in your mercy,
    hear our prayer.

Lord of all,
    give wisdom to all who work for peace,
    so that a more secure future may be ensured for all.
Give courage to those who strive for justice,
    so that the causes of conflict may be overcome.
Give strength to those who seek to break down barriers,
    so that divisions over race, colour, creed and culture may be ended.
Grant that wherever war, or the threat of war, continues to haunt lives,

a way of reconciliation may be found,
and harmony established between people and nations.
Lord, in your mercy,
hear our prayer.
In the name of Christ.
Amen.

Hymn   *The King shall come when morning breaks*
Forth in the peace of Christ we go

Closing prayer
Living God,
again we bring you our prayer:
your kingdom come,
your will be done,
on earth as it is in heaven.
Amen.

CHURCH ANNIVERSARY (1)

Possible visual and music material

Transparencies for this service will be difficult to find, but are there perhaps old photographs of your town, church building and former members that you could have converted into slides and shown at some point in the service? A suitable piece of music to which these could be set is the Beatles classic *Yesterday*.

Introduction

Another anniversary, another year in the life of this church – that is what we have gathered here today to celebrate, but, of course, the history of this fellowship is but one speck on a much broader canvas, reaching back to the days of the early Church following the death and resurrection of Christ. It is there that we shall start our reflections today, remembering the work of the Apostle Paul in taking the gospel beyond the confines of Judea and out into the wider world. It is to his vision that we in large part owe our being here today, and his single-minded determination to proclaim Christ affords a continuing challenge. From Paul, we will move on to a more general consideration of remembering the past, reminding ourselves that such remembering should serve as a springboard to the future rather than a barricade against it. Finally, we will turn to the pages of the Old Testament and God's call of Abram to venture out into the unknown; a call he makes in various ways to all those who are serious about serving him. We will move, then, by degrees from what *has been* to what *shall be,* and as we do so let us pray that God will help us, as individuals and a fellowship, to do the same.

Hymn   *Lord, for the years your love has kept and guided*
Your hand, O God, has guided

Prayer
Sovereign God,
   Lord of past, present and future,
   Lord of all,

we come together, as we have come so often across the years,
to thank and praise you.

We come rejoicing that, in all the uncertainties of life,
we find in you one who is unchanging,
a rock on which we can base our lives,
a shield to protect us along the way,
a light to guide our footsteps
and a love that fills our hearts with joy.
You have been our dwelling-place in all generations.
From everlasting to everlasting you are God.

We come to praise you for all the ways you have blessed us,
as individuals and as a church –
for the times of fellowship we have shared,
the faith that has been nurtured,
the support given and received,
and the friendships established.
You have been our dwelling-place in all generations.
From everlasting to everlasting you are God.

We praise you for the experiences we have gone through together –
the hopes realised,
disappointments overcome,
lessons learned,
service offered.
You have been our dwelling-place in all generations.
From everlasting to everlasting you are God.

Forgive us that we are slow sometimes to remember your goodness
and swift to forget your many blessings.
We lose sight of the resources you put at our disposal,
dwelling on our fears rather than your strength,
our problems rather than your promises,
our lives rather than your kingdom.
We become wrapped up in what is unimportant,
putting our trust in what finally cannot satisfy,
our energy into what ultimately is secondary to our calling.
Our love, faith and commitment ebb and flow as each day passes,
yet still you have been with us,
rich in mercy and grace.
You have been our dwelling-place in all generations.
From everlasting to everlasting you are God.

Receive our thanks that you are so different from us –
    faithful,
    constant,
    unchanging,
    always willing to show mercy,
    forever reaching out in love.
Receive our praise that you have been able to work through our lives,
    despite as well as because of us.
You have been our dwelling-place in all generations.
From everlasting to everlasting you are God.

Sovereign God,
    help us to recognise that, though all else may fail, you will not,
    and may that knowledge shape our life together.
Help us to build on all that has gone before,
    so that we may follow you more faithfully,
    love you more truly,
    and see more clearly what you would have us do.
You have been our dwelling-place in all generations.
From everlasting to everlasting you are God.
To you be praise and glory,
    now and for evermore,
    through Jesus Christ our Lord.
Amen.

Comment

How must Paul have felt towards the end of his life as he looked back over his ministry and saw what God had done through him? We cannot know for sure, but there are enough reminiscences in his letters to make plain the obstacles he was up against and the sense of wonder he felt at God being able to use him despite them all. For example, we will listen in a moment to words from his letter to the Galatians that graphically illustrate how unlikely a choice he was to proclaim the gospel. Yet what must surely have seemed impossible to him proved possible for God. No doubt those who started this church faced their own obstacles in turn, just as we encounter difficulties in our journey of discipleship. We may sometimes feel the challenge is beyond us. Paul's words remind us that it is not *us* we are talking about, but God!

Reading: Galatians 1:13-24

Meditation of Paul

It looked impossible at the beginning,
    utterly beyond me.
And I don't mind confessing there were many times
    when I felt like giving up,
    throwing in the towel and cutting my losses.
Surprised?
You shouldn't be.
After all, just look what I was up against –
    me, Paul, called to take the gospel beyond Jerusalem,
    beyond Judea,
    out to the ends of the earth!
It was a tall order by anyone's reckoning,
    and when you remember how the Jews felt about Gentiles,
    and how the Gentiles felt in return,
    well, you can begin to understand the scale of the problem, can't you!
I was up against it from the very start,
    doing my best to keep a foot in both camps to avoid causing offence,
    trying to share the good news,
    but forever keeping one eye over my shoulder,
    knowing the snipers wouldn't be far away.
It didn't help, I suppose, with my own people anyway,
    me being a Jew myself,
    schooled as a Pharisee and expert in the Law to boot!
They thought I was betraying my roots,
    reneging on my convictions,
    denying the faith of our fathers.
And as for the Gentiles, many simply wondered what I was doing
    pushing my nose into their affairs.
So, yes, I had my doubts, to put it mildly!
Wouldn't you have felt the same?
Who was I to overcome that sort of prejudice,
    to break down the barriers between us,
    to bring people of such contrasting backgrounds together
    into one family of humankind?
Who was I to talk of a new way of thinking,
    of building a different sort of kingdom,
    of sharing a different sort of love?
Someone else perhaps – but me?
No way!
And yet the mystery is I did!
Somehow, in a way I'll never understand,

I found the strength and the words I needed when I needed them most.
I found energy to begin new tasks,
    courage to meet new people,
    faith to dream new dreams.
I unearthed reserves I never knew existed,
    and achieved results I never imagined possible –
    all kinds of people,
    in all kinds of ways,
    discovering the joy of sharing and working together,
    discovering a faith that answered their deepest needs –
    a faith to live by.
It looked impossible, you can't argue with that –
    wonderful yet altogether ridiculous.
But it wasn't,
    for I've discovered since then,
    much to my amazement,
    much to my relief,
    that I can do all things
    through him who strengthens me.
Thanks be to God!

Silent reflection

Prayer
Sovereign God,
    the challenges you set before us may seem small
    compared with those faced by others over the years,
    but they can seem daunting nonetheless.
We feel inadequate to meet the task,
    acutely conscious of our lack of faith,
    the limitations of our gifts
    and our inability to serve you as we would wish.
Yet, time and again throughout history
    you have taken the most unpromising of material
    and used it in ways defying all expectations.
You have turned doubt into faith,
    weakness into strength,
    timid service into fearless discipleship,
    and you go on doing that today
    through the power of your Holy Spirit.
Give us, then, faith to respond to your call,
    trusting that, whatever you ask of us,

you will be by our side to help us see it through,
to the glory of your name.
Amen.

Comment

Two things have always fascinated people. One is the past and the other
is the future. Today, those probably fascinate us more than ever. We have
shops devoted to selling re-creations of historical artefacts, a host of tele-
vision documentaries concerning key moments in history, and numerous
tourist attractions, museums and theme parks focusing upon bygone
days. On the other hand, issues such as global warming, possible meteor
strikes, genetic engineering and technology constantly exercise the brains
of academics and ordinary people alike as they ponder the implications
of such things for this and future generations. Both the past and the
future have much to teach us, so long as we use them to illuminate rather
than blot out the present. We cannot afford to lose ourselves in nostalgic
yearnings for the good old days. On the other hand, we must not pin all
our hopes on the future, nor allow fears concerning what might one day
happen to so dominate our lives that we think of nothing else. We need
to remember that we serve Jesus Christ, the same yesterday, today and
tomorrow, and the God who is before all and beyond all.

Reading: Psalm 42:1-11

Meditation (to be read by two voices)

Why did it have to end, Lord?
We'd worked so hard to reach that moment,
    to achieve something lasting and worthwhile,
    and life was good,
    as we'd always hoped it might be.
Not perfect, of course,
    for there were still problems to face and work to be done,
    but we were happy,
    at peace with ourselves,
    at one with the world.
And we gave our all,
    gladly,
    joyfully,
    wanting nothing,
    having everything.
I know I shouldn't indulge in nostalgia,
    but I can't help it, Lord,

for it was the best time of my life,
and I want to go back to the good old days,
the way things used to be,
for I never realised at the time how special they were,
or how much they meant.
I do now, though, all too clearly,
and my heart aches with the memories –
the moments we shared,
the people we knew,
the pleasure we gave,
the joy we received.
It was good, Lord,
a precious, priceless time –
why did it have to end?

My child,
there's nothing wrong with nostalgia, never think that.
You've experienced much,
and it's right to recall it,
to reflect on the good times,
to remember the past.
But to try to *live* there, that *would* be wrong,
a squandering of the past and denial of the future,
for what's here today is gone tomorrow,
what one moment is certain the next may be shaken.
You're surrounded by change,
each moment,
each day,
nothing, however precious,
however solid,
safe from the passage of time.
Nothing, that is, except my word,
my purpose,
and my love.
It's in these you must put trust,
where hope alone must rest,
for though heaven and earth may pass away
these will never change.
Look back with thanks,
look forward with hope;
remember the past,
reach out for the future,

for I offer love that endures for ever,
and joy that will never end,
in this life, or the next.

Silent reflection

Hymn   *One more step along the world I go*
           Will you come and follow me?

Prayer of intercession

Loving God,
  we give you thanks for our church here,
  remembering all we have shared together
  and looking forward to everything the future still holds.
Hear now our prayer for your people in every place.
Grant your blessing upon their life and witness,
  and upon all you have called to service.
Build up your Church
  and so bring closer your kingdom.

We pray for those involved in mission, either at home or overseas –
  evangelists,
  preachers,
  chaplains,
  missionaries,
  all those who seek to proclaim the gospel
  and make known the love of Christ.
Build up your Church
  and so bring closer your kingdom.

We pray for those who exercise roles of leadership,
  whether it be over individual fellowships,
  dioceses,
  districts,
  associations,
  denominations,
  or ecumenical groupings.
Build up your Church
  and so bring closer your kingdom.

We pray for those who witness to you in their daily life and work,
  expressing their faith in all kinds of occupations and vocations,
  fleshing out the gospel, putting it into practice,

exploring what it means in concrete and sometimes difficult situations.
Build up your Church
and so bring closer your kingdom.

We pray for those who work for Christian unity,
striving to draw your divided Church together,
breaking down barriers
and building bridges of trust, respect, and co-operation.
Build up your Church
and so bring closer your kingdom.

Loving God,
guide your people,
strengthen, equip and inspire each one for service,
and so may we, with them, joyfully serve you,
sensitively proclaim you,
and faithfully express your love for all.
Build up your Church
and so bring closer your kingdom.
Through Jesus Christ our Lord.
Amen.

Comment

To venture out into the unknown, unsure of where we are going or what
we will find when we get there – how many of us would be willing to do
that? Thankfully, far less will be asked of most of us, but this is the faith
Abram was willing to show and that paved the way for the unfolding of
God's sovereign purpose. We may not be asked to show anything like
such trust, but God does expect us to seek his will rather than our own
and to be open to his guidance rather than simply pursue our own plans.
We do not know what the future holds but we know who holds the
future. Are we willing to step out in faith if, and when, he asks us?

Reading: Genesis 12:1-5

Meditation of Abram

Hang on a minute, I said,
let's get this straight:
you're not serious, surely?
A trifle familiar you might say,
and you'd be right, I realise that now,
but at the time I'd no idea who I was talking to,
just this inner conviction

that I should pick up sticks and head off to goodness knows where,
   and start again.
It was a lot to ask, wasn't it? –
   enough to make anyone in their right mind think twice.
Yet that's how it was for me,
   just this voice in my head
   telling me to pack my bags and head off into the wilderness,
   away to a land he would show me.
Was I simply restless, I wondered –
   the years bringing with them the urge to move on?
But no, it wasn't that –
   deep down I knew, despite the doubts,
   that God was speaking to me –
   God as I'd never known him,
   never imagined him,
   never encountered him before.
And I was hooked, pure and simple,
   for here was a God unlike any other –
   mighty,
   majestic,
   mysterious –
   not *shaped* by our hands but *shaping* our lives,
   not *ours* to control but controlling *all*;
   a God beyond expression,
   sovereign over history,
   ruler over heaven and earth.
It was exhilarating and terrifying,
   a moment of promise, yet also of dread,
   for here was a call to leave home and livelihood,
   to tear up roots and forsake everything familiar –
   then venture out into the unknown.
Do you realise what that meant?
It wasn't just *me* involved, but my loved ones,
   them too asked to make the sacrifice and take the step of faith –
   a lot to expect of anyone,
   even had we known the way ahead.
Yet they agreed,
   willingly,
   gladly,
   without a moment's hesitation,
   for they saw, so they told me, a light in my eyes
   and a flame in my heart,

like nothing they'd seen before.
It was a hard journey,
    longer than we ever expected,
    with many a trial and tribulation along the way,
    but there were blessings too,
    surprises I could never have dreamt of,
    and the greatest of all
    is the lesson I've learned never to fear the future,
    for however uncertain it may be,
    and whatever it may bring,
    I realise now we must keep on travelling,
    journeying in faith,
    until our dying day.

Prayer of petition

Lord,
    you do not call us to a destination but a journey,
    a journey of continual new discoveries
    and new experiences of your love.
Save us from ever thinking we have arrived,
    from imagining we know all there is to know,
    or that we have exhausted the riches of everything you would reveal to us.
Open our eyes to the great adventure of life
    and to the unfathomable mysteries of your purpose,
    and so help us to be a pilgrim people,
    travelling in faith as Abraham travelled before us,
    until we reach at last the kingdom you hold in store for all your people.
Amen.

Hymn   *Lord, as we rise to leave this shell of worship*
              Forth in the name of Christ we go

Closing prayer

Remember all God has done.
Rejoice in all he is doing.
Receive all he shall yet do.
Put your hand in his,
    the God of past, present and future,
    and walk with him wherever he may lead,
    knowing that he will walk with you,
    this day and always.
Amen.

Church Anniversary (2)

Possible visual and music material   See suggestion for Church Anniversary (1).

Introduction   Few of us like change. We may think we do. We may imagine that, unlike former generations, we are open to new ideas and safe from becoming stuck in a rut, but the fact is that all of us, as the years go by, develop attachments to particular ways of doing things, and we find any alterations to these difficult to accept. Churches are no exception. We grow used to a hymn book, version of the Bible, minister, meeting, pattern of worship and so much else, to the point that we give such things a sanctity of their own. Yet change is inevitable, painful though it may be. While it must not dilute its central message, the Church must nonetheless adapt or die. This is not to say we should welcome change for change's sake, nor that we should abandon all of the old in favour of the new, but we must be ready to build on the past and, where necessary, to let go and embrace the future. Cling to what has been and we may find ourselves closing the door to what God has yet to do.

Hymn   *For I'm building a people of power*
Christ, of the upward way

Prayer

Loving God,
    on this day of thanksgiving and celebration
    we praise you for who and what you are.
We marvel at your great goodness,
    the love and care, mercy and forgiveness
    you have so faithfully shown;
    the strength, support, guidance and inspiration you have so freely given.
We praise you for all you have done for us –
    the lessons we have learned,
    the blessings we have received,
    the faith that has grown.

We praise you for everything you shall yet do among us –
    all that life continues to offer,
    all we have still to attempt and experience,
    and that you hold in store for us in the years ahead,
    and on into eternity.
Loving God,
    for all you are,
    all you have been,
    and all you shall be,
    we praise you,
In the name of Christ.
Amen.

Comment

When is it right to hold on to the past and when should we let go? There is no easy answer to that question, for every situation is different. At times, we have to accept that the life of something is over. On other occasions, we need to beware of throwing out what has served us well for the sake of the untried and untested. At other times still, we must learn to accommodate the past while adapting it to a new situation. As we listen now to words of Jesus concerning the old and new, and then to a meditation upon them, ask yourself what his words mean for you and for the life of our fellowship here.

Readings: Mark 2:21-22 and Matthew 13:52

Meditation of Nicodemus, Pharisee turned follower of Christ

He was right, of course,
    it doesn't do to mix the old with the new;
    try that and you risk losing both.
Only it's one thing applying that to wine or pieces of cloth,
    quite another when it comes to faith,
    the gulf between them and the implications involved world's apart.
Yet that's what he seemed to be suggesting
    through that illustration of his –
    a break with the past,
    a parting of the ways,
    a revolution in our thinking.
That took some getting used to,
    for everything we held dear was rooted in history,
    built up over the centuries,

a priceless tradition of which we were justly proud.
Little wonder that some took offence at his words.
How could we throw it all aside?
It was too much to ask.
It would have been, too,
   had that been what he meant,
   but it wasn't,
   things not quite that simple after all.
'Do not think I have come to abolish the law or the prophets,' he said.
   'I have come not to abolish but to fulfil.
   Truly I tell you,
   until heaven and earth pass away,
   not one letter,
   not one stroke of a letter,
   will pass from the Law until all is accomplished.'
You can't get much clearer than that, can you?
No, he wasn't destroying the Law,
   so much as reinterpreting it,
   getting down to its true meaning;
   and that meant moving on in our understanding,
   broadening our horizons,
   recognising that the way of Christ could not be tied down
   to what had gone before.
The old had its place and always would have,
   a lamp to our people across the centuries
   which still had power to speak,
   but a new light had dawned,
   a new beginning,
   which inevitably meant change;
   not just in the trimmings of religion –
   ritual, ceremony and observance –
   but in every part of life,
   body, mind and soul.
He called us to put off the old self and put on the new,
   to start afresh,
   be born again,
   for only then can we share in the wine he brings.
It's painful to let go, I know,
   to put behind you what is so familiar
   that it has almost become part of you,
   and, believe me, I'm struggling with it as much as anyone.
But he's helped me to see that there's no other way,

no other option that will do,
for if we cling to the past,
not only will we lose sight of the present,
we will never embrace the future.

Silent reflection

Prayer

Lord Jesus Christ,
  we are not good at letting go of the past,
  at recognising there are times when we need to move on in life
  and take a step forward in faith if we are ever truly to grow.
We prefer the security of the familiar,
  the comfort of that which does not stretch or challenge us too far,
  and we are wary of the prospect of change,
  afraid that it might ask more of us than we are willing to give.
We are not good at letting go of the old and putting on the new,
  at turning away from our former way of life
  and taking instead the way of the cross,
  at trusting in your guidance and walking in the power of your Spirit.
We are reluctant to abandon old habits,
  fearful of being thought different,
  unwilling to deny ourselves the pleasures of this world
  for the promise of the world to come.
So we try to keep a foot in both camps,
  to combine the old self with the new.
We think we can balance the two,
  but, of course, we can't,
  the end result being to compromise both and embrace neither.
Help us to understand that, while the old has its place,
  there are some areas in life where a complete break is needed,
  a turning away from what *has been*
  before we are ready to receive what *shall be*.
Lord Jesus Christ,
  you want to work within us
  to finish the new creation you have begun.
Give us courage to trust you completely,
  so that you may refashion our lives to your glory.
We ask it in your name.
Amen.

Comment

It is often remarked that even the best-laid plans go to waste, and we will all know from experience how true that is. We do our best to plan for the future, carefully considering the various options open to us, but there are other forces in play that are beyond our control. Life has an uncomfortable habit of upsetting the apple-cart just when we think we've got it under control. That is not to say we should not make plans, for sensible steward-ship requires that we look to the future, but as we do so we need always to seek God's will, discerning as far as possible his purpose rather than our own. It is equally important that we are open to the possibility that we have got things wrong; that God is seeking to lead us in a new direction that flies in the face of all that has gone before. God will not force our hand, and we will not always respond as we should, but thankfully, though we may sometimes frustrate his purpose, he is always ready to start from where we find ourselves and lead us forward.

Proverbs 16:1, 9; 19:21; 20:24; Jeremiah 10:23

Meditation (to be read by two voices)

I've got it all planned, Lord,
   down to the very last detail,
   everything mapped out just as I want it to be.
And it's marvellous to know at long last where I stand,
   to have a clear idea of where I'm going and what I want.
It's been a long time coming –
   for most of my life I've just drifted along
   with no sense of purpose,
   and little hope for the future,
   content simply to get by as best I can,
   avoiding the pitfalls,
   making the best of the good times,
   holding on through the bad.
Even when I had a clearer picture –
   a vision to work towards,
   a dream to aim for –
   all too often that was thwarted,
   life twisting and turning,
   wriggling off the line,
   just when I thought I had it under control.
But suddenly it's all changed,
   everything finally slotting into place,

and this time, Lord, it will be different –
no mistakes,
no letting the prize slip through my fingers –
I know what I want,
and I'm going to reach out to make it mine.

My child,
    what are you saying?
After all you've been through, you know life's not that simple.
I'm glad you're excited,
    for it's good to look forward,
    to dream dreams,
    to have hopes,
    but don't get carried away,
    or you'll fall over yourself in your hurry.
You can't control the future;
    it's in my hands,
    and if that's hard to live with sometimes,
    not knowing what the next day might bring,
    ask yourself this:
    would you really want it any different?
You may think so,
    but consider the responsibility involved,
    the decisions to be taken,
    the choices to be made,
    each affecting not just you
    but the lives of those around you.
And could you know today what you will want tomorrow,
    the way your thoughts might change,
    your tastes evolve,
    your aspirations alter as the years go by?
I doubt it,
    but assuming you could,
    just imagine a life with no surprises,
    closed to the unexpected,
    everything running precisely to plan –
    is that how you'd like to live?
No, my child, it's not you who holds the future,
    it's me;
    and though you may wish it were different,
    though it's hard sometimes to accept,
    there's nowhere better to leave it.

Silent reflection

Hymn   *Church of God, elect and glorious*
We thank you for the memories

Comment

Above all, our purpose today in celebrating another year in the life of this church is to seek God's guidance for the path he would have us take in the years ahead. It is easy to say that, much harder for us to mean business, for when God speaks we may not always like what we hear. He may ask of us more than we feel able to give, lead us in a direction we would rather not go, and call of us to move on from things we would rather hold on to. Yet whatever God asks of us, he will give us strength to do, and wherever he asks us to go, he will be there by our sides. As we remember what he has done in past generations, are we truly ready to open our lives to what he would say and do among us, here and now?

Reading: Hebrews 4:12-16

Meditation (to be read by two voices)

God, I asked you to speak,
   and you spoke,
   and I wish now I'd kept quiet,
   for your word is frightening,
   challenging,
   demanding,
   disturbing.
It breaks into my comfortable complacency,
   it upsets my quiet composure,
   it questions my willingness to compromise,
   it threatens my hard-won confidence.
God, I asked you to speak,
   and you spoke,
   and now I'm asking you, help me to listen,
   to accept,
   and to respond.

My child,
   it's come as a shock, hasn't it,
   this answer I've given?
But it shouldn't have done,
   not if your prayer was genuine.

You looked to me for guidance,
   and I gave it;
   not perhaps what you wanted to hear,
   nor what you expected,
   but what you asked for nonetheless –
   my word to you,
   searching,
   rebuking,
   renewing.
It's up to you now, what you make of it.
You can close your ears and turn away,
   pretending you never heard me,
   or in faith you can face my challenge
   and find light for your path,
   food for your soul,
   the word that offers life.

Silent reflection

Prayer of thanksgiving and petition

Gracious God,
   we thank you today
   for all who have contributed to the life of this church.

We remember those who have served as ministers,
   thanking you for the guidance, leadership
   and pastoral care each has offered.
God of past, present and future,
   hear our prayer.

We remember those who have held positions of responsibility
   within this fellowship,
   thanking you for the faithful work
   they have performed among us.
God of past, present and future,
   hear our prayer.

We think of those who have worked behind the scenes, often unnoticed,
   thanking you for the vital contribution
   they have made to our life together.
God of past, present and future,
   hear our prayer.

We think of those whose vision it was to first start this church,
    thanking you for the labour and sacrifice
    that went into turning that dream into reality.
God of past, present and future,
    hear our prayer.

We think of those who in a multitude of ways
    have shared their faith with others,
    thanking you for all who have come to know you as a result.
God of past, present and future,
    hear our prayer.

We think of all we have known in this church,
    enriching us by their presence,
    and we thank you for the example of their faith and commitment.
God of past, present and future,
    hear our prayer.

Teach us to build on the heritage you have given us.
Save us from ever growing complacent,
    from becoming a people with no vision,
    content simply to keep our doors open.
God of past, present and future,
    hear our prayer.

Save us from becoming closed to all that is new and different,
    from turning in on ourselves,
    or from being divided in our goals.
God of past, present and future,
    hear our prayer.

Give us a vision of the way you can use us.
Help us to dream of what your Church can be,
    and to work towards that dream's fulfilment.
God of past, present and future,
    hear our prayer.

Gracious God,
    for all that has been done,
    and all that shall be done,
    we give you our thanks,
    trusting in your continued blessing.

God of past, present and future,
   hear our prayer.
In the name of Christ.
Amen.

Hymn   *When the Church of Jesus*
           The Church of Christ in every age

Closing prayer

God, go with us on our journey of faith –
   revive us when we grow weary,
   direct us when we go astray,
   inspire us when we lose heart,
   reprove us when we turn back.

Keep us travelling ever-onwards;
   a pilgrim people,
   looking to Jesus Christ
   who has run the race before us,
   and who waits to welcome us home.
Amen.

Appendix

- *Jesus of Nazareth*
  Colour transparencies from the TV series directed by Franco Zeffirelli. Was produced by *The Bible Society* but is no longer available commercially.

- *The Life of Christ*
  Slides produced by: *Visual Publications*, The Green, Northleach, Cheltenham, Gloucestershire GL54 3EX. Tel 01451 860519

- *Fountain of Life* (Margaret Rizza)
  CD and cassette produced by Kevin Mayhew Publishers.